ISBN 978-1-332-06944-6
PIBN 10279927

1 MONTH OF
FREE
READING

at

www.ForgottenBooks.com

By purchasing this book you are eligible for one month membership to ForgottenBooks.com, giving you unlimited access to our entire collection of over 1,000,000 titles via our web site and mobile apps.

To claim your free month visit:

www.forgottenbooks.com/free279927

English
Français
Deutsche
Italiano
Español
Português

www.forgottenbooks.com

Mythology Photography **Fiction**
Fishing Christianity **Art** Cooking
Essays Buddhism Freemasonry
Medicine **Biology** Music **Ancient
Egypt** Evolution Carpentry Physics
Dance Geology **Mathematics** Fitness
Shakespeare **Folklore** Yoga Marketing
Confidence Immortality Biographies
Poetry **Psychology** Witchcraft
Electronics Chemistry History **Law**
Accounting **Philosophy** Anthropology
Alchemy Drama Quantum Mechanics
Atheism Sexual Health **Ancient History**
Entrepreneurship Languages Sport
Paleontology Needlework Islam
Metaphysics Investment Archaeology
Parenting Statistics Criminology
Motivational

THE
CHARLES LARNED
MEMORIAL

OXFORD

MASSACHUSETTS

1906

CHARLES LARNED MEMORIAL.

FRONT VIEW, FROM THE NORTH-EAST.

SOUVENIR

OF THE

CHARLES LARNED MEMORIAL

AND THE

FREE PUBLIC LIBRARY

OXFORD, MASSACHUSETTS

1906

BOSTON
GEO. H. ELLIS CO., PRINTERS, 272 CONGRESS STREET
1906

FOREWORD.

The prime object of the following pages is to report the dedicatory exercises of the

CHARLES LARNED MEMORIAL,

but its character as a memorial and as a working factor in the individual and social life of the community cannot be fully appreciated without a somewhat detailed account of its history and structural features, while the only fitting introduction thereto is a brief sketch of the

FREE PUBLIC LIBRARY

whose needs called it into being and with which henceforth it is to be identified. This sketch has been extracted from the Town Report of 1890, which with all other material has been selected and arranged for this brochure, that, as far as limits would permit, it might at least approach completeness and symmetry.

BENEFACTORS

OF THE

FREE PUBLIC LIBRARY.

1868.
HON. IRA M. BARTON, FOUNDER,
$1000.

1876.
HON. GEORGE L. DAVIS,
$500.

1892.
GEN. NELSON H. DAVIS,
$250.

1895.
MRS. MARY S. T. WALLACE,
$1993.25.

1898.
JEREMIAH LEARNED, ESQ.,
Residuary Portion of Estate.

1902.
ORRIN F. JOSLIN, ESQ.,
$1000.
TOWN OF OXFORD,
$4500.
For Purchase of Present Site.

1904.
MISS MATTIE E. SAWTELLE,
$700.

HON. RICHARD OLNEY,
$1000.
CHARLES LARNED, ESQ.,
The "Charles Larned Memorial."

CHARLES LARNED MEMORIAL.

REAR VIEW, FROM THE SOUTH WEST.

EXTRACT FROM THE REPORT

ON THE

FREE PUBLIC LIBRARY.

1890.

In the belief that everything contributing to the formation of our own Free Public Library would be of interest, a brief historical sketch of this and kindred enterprises preceding it has been compiled from material kindly furnished by Mr. George F. Daniels.

PASTOR'S LIBRARY.

The first collection of books in Oxford, constituting a library of perhaps not over ten volumes, was contributed, some as early as 1719, by Paul Dudley, Rev. Benjamin Wadsworth, and other gentlemen of Boston and vicinity, well-wishers of the town, for the use of the minister. Several of these volumes were preserved as late as 1840, in the receptacle of the "Social Library," which was formed later. Among them were specimens of costly book-making, ponderous volumes, books of sermons, commentaries, and prolix treatises on religious subjects. Some volumes are still in existence, two of which contain interesting inscriptions. The first, being a Scripture Commentary printed in London in 1624, was in 1701 the property of Mr. Wadsworth, minister of the First Church in Boston, once President of Harvard College. On the margin of the first leaf is written "For Oxford Library," opposite, on the blank page, "The gift of the Rev'd Mr. Benjamin Wadsworth—for the use of the Church or Parish Library of Oxford in the County of Suffolk, 1719." The other is entitled "Hexapla," or Commentary on Romans. On the back of this title-page is written "Roxbury, 3d July, 1736. For the use of the Parish Library in Oxford, New England, the Rev. Mr. Cambel being the present minister. Given by Paul Dudley." There was also a large folio in Latin, being "An Exposition of the Psalms, given by Rev. Dr. Colman," a volume of Sermons by Samuel Hieron, given by Samuel Taylor of Boston, and one written by William Morice, Esq., given by Paul Dudley.*

*A receipt of Deacon Samuel Harris, 15 Nov. 1784, indicates that five volumes at least had been in the custody of Rev. Joseph Bowman, and were at that date delivered up to the church; described as "one folio in Latin, an Exposition of the Psalms, and four other small folios in English, being Hieron's Sermons, one written by Samuel Morice, Esq., one a Sixfold Commentary on Romans, and the fourth a Commentary on Proverbs and Psalms."

(These volumes were finally given to the Free Public Library by the First Congregational Church. See Town Reports for 1890-91.)

SOCIAL LIBRARY

The second, called the "Social Library," was established about the time of the Revolutionary War. It was founded through the influence of Josiah Wolcott, Dr. Stephen Barton, Jonathan Davis, and others, and was an important institution of the village during the latter part of the last century. Its early records are lost. It was at first a stock company, and the proceeds of the sales of shares were expended in purchasing books. Donations of books were also made by individuals. Its depository was, for many years, at the Butler tavern. Later it was removed to the dwelling-house of Peter Butler, in whose care it remained until his decease in 1857. A catalogue and list of members, dated 1 March, 1818, gives 113 volumes and 30 proprietors. Total cost of books, $254.27.*

* In 1839 Judge Barton, then of Worcester, presented to the library four large Supplementary Volumes of the British Encyclopædia with a volume of plates. In his accompanying note addressed to Mr. Peter Butler, he says, "In tendering it to your Association, I shall only make a small but grateful return for the pleasure and benefit derived in the days of my boyhood from their useful library."

(These volumes, together with Vol. VIII. of Rollin's Ancient History, passed into the hands of Mrs. John Pratt of Oxford, who gave them to the Free Public Library. See Town Reports for 1890–91.)

The Catalogue was as follows: British Album, Brown's Elements, Barclay's Apology, Chesterfield Abridged, Clark's Travels, 3 vols., Campbell's Narrative, Dean's Husbandry, Dialogue of Devils, Domestic Encyclopædia, 5 vols., Domestic Cookery, Encyclopædia, 18 vols., Franklin's Works, Female Biography, Goldsmith's Works, 6 vols., Grandpré's Voyage, Holmes' Sketches, 2 vols, The Hive, Herriot's Travels, Heathen Gods, Indian Wars, Locke on the Understanding, 2 vols., Life of Washington, 5 vols., Paradise Lost, Memoir of Cumberland, Modern Europe, Prideaux' History of the Bible, 4 vols., Parent's Friend, Pope's Works, 4 vols., Parke's Travels, Porteus' Evidences of Christian Religion, Relly's Works, 2 vols., Rights of Women, Rambler, 4 vols, Rollin's Ancient History, 8 vols., Robertson's America, 2 vols., Seneca's Morals, Self Knowledge, Shakespeare, 6 vols., Spectator, 8 vols., The Task, Thomson's Seasons, Telemachus, 2 vols., Thinks I to Myself,

It is known that in 1841 some shareholders drew out their proportion of books permanently, but not nearly all did so; and on 7 March, 1859, the balance of the collection was sold at auction to Mr. Daniel Rich for $8.55, and the books were scattered in all directions.

SOCIETY LIBRARY.

In January, 1792, the Congregational Church voted an appropriation of £30 from the Hagburn fund toward a new library. Mr. Dudley seems to have been the prime mover in this matter, and with Captain Elisha Davis, Deacon John Dana, and Captain Ebenezer Humphrey was deputed to buy books. The record recites: "The following are the conditions on which the church agrees to lay out money ... in junction with other gentlemen subscribers in the town." The following, outside the church, paid each 15 shillings and were members: John Ballard, Jonas Eddy, Lemuel Crane, Anthony Sigourney, Simeon Kingsbury, Ebenezer Shumway, Jr., Jesse Stone of Ward, Allen Hancock, Amos Shumway, Jr., Joseph Hurd, Daniel Kingsbury, Ambrose Stone, Jr., Sylvanus Town. Sigourney sold in 1796 to Elias Pratt.

Vicar of Wakefield, Views of Religion, Whitney's History of Worcester County, Mr. Williams' Letters, Winchester's Letters.

The names of the proprietors were as follows: James Butler, Peter Butler, Lemuel Crane, Jonathan Davis, Rufus Davis, Abijah Davis, Nehemiah Davis, Stephen Davis, Jonathan Davis, Jr., William T. Fisk, Asa Harris, Samuel Harris, Jonas Hartwell, Bradford Hudson, Jeremiah Kingsbury, Samuel Kingsbury, Stephen Kingsbury, Sylvanus Learned, Abisha Learned, William Lamson, John Mayo, Richard Moore, Thomas Meriam, Jotham Meriam, John Pratt, John Putnam, Amos Rich, Joseph Stone, William Sigourney, Samuel Ward.

In February, 1792, books to the value of £27 14s. were bought, and the library was soon opened. According to the by-laws, the pastor, Mr. Dudley, was librarian, acting efficiently while he remained in town.*

The library opened with about 80 volumes. Later, from time to time, additions were made by gift and purchase, so that the aggregate was probably nearly or quite 150 volumes. It is no slight compliment to the intelligence, character, and good taste of the members of the church and this association that, as the records testify, these solid volumes were, for many years, extensively circulated and read throughout the town.

A prudential committee of five was chosen annually to manage the general affairs of the institution, and for the first twenty years the following constituted this committee: Ebenezer Learned, Elisha Davis, Samuel Harris, Samuel Crane, John Ballard,

---

*The titles of works first purchased were: Gibbon's Abridgment, 2 vols., Robertson's America, 2 vols, Guthrie's Grammar, Morse's Grammar, Dodd's Thoughts, Fordyce's Sermons, Paley's Philosophy, Citizen of the World, 2 vols., Blackstone's Commentaries, 4 vols., Webster's Essay, Paradise Lost, Night Thoughts, Beattie's Evidences, Beattie's Moral Science, Stackhouse's History of the Bible, 6 vols, The Task, Edwards on the Will, Jennyn's View, Mason's Self Knowledge, Watts' Death and Heaven, Ramsay's History, Doddridge's Rise and Progress, Child's Friend, 2 vols, Minot's Insurrections, Keats' Pelew Islands, Vicar of Wakefield, Edwards on Sin, Edwards on Redemption, Gardiner's Life, Blair's Sermons, 2 vols., Boston's Distinguished Characters, Edwards on the Affections, Edwards against Chauncey, The Spectator, 8 vols., Doddridge's Sermons, Christian Theology, Pilgrim's Progress, Martin's Grammar, Newton on the Prophecies, 2 vols, Seneca's Morals, Hopkins on Holiness, Edwards on Virtue, American Preacher, 3 vols., Butler's Analogy, Price's Dissertations, Hervey's Meditations, Bigelow's Tour, 2 vols., Millot's Elements, 5 vols., Locke's Essay, 2 vols, Ferguson's Astronomy.

(The remnant of this library was given to the Free Public Library by the First Congregational Church. See Town Reports for 1890-91.)

Ebenezer Humphrey, Joseph Hurd, Joshua Turner, John Dana.

On Mr. Dudley's removal in 1799, Jonathan Harris was chosen librarian, and continued until January, 1806, when Rev. J. Moulton became *ex-officio* the custodian. He only retained it till April, when Col. Sylvanus Town was elected, serving until the settlement of Mr. Batcheller in 1816, who assumed charge. He died October, 1822; and January, 1823, Calvin Perry was librarian, at which time interest had much declined. In January, 1825, the church voted sixty dollars to replenish the collection, and Seth Daniels was chosen librarian. About this time the name was changed from "Society Library" to "Second Social Library." Among the important additions at this time were Scott's Bible, 6 volumes, Rollin's History in several volumes, Silliman's Travels, 3 volumes, Massillon's Sermons, Kimpton's History of the Bible.

In July, 1831, the books were removed to the custody of John Wetherell, where they continued two or three years at least, and later, a proposition being made for a removal to the new meeting-house, as being more central, they were taken to the vestibule of the gallery, where they remained until the removal of the house to its present location, when they were put in the basement, where they have since remained.

After the removal of the library to the church, having no responsible custodian, it was but little used; and, being in a public place, many volumes disappeared, so that at present only about twenty-five remain. The case is now used by the Sunday School.*

LIBRARY ASSOCIATION.

This was an organization of the young people, numbering fifty or more, formed in 1856. While its ultimate object was to establish a library, it first took the form of a reading club, meeting at private houses once in two weeks. Conducted by its members, there was a literary paper called the *Evening Star*. An effort was made to raise funds by lectures, but was relinquished. In December a dramatic entertainment was given at Sanford's Hall, which put more than fifty dollars into the treasury, which with membership fees, fines, etc., enabled the Society in December, 1857, to buy 84 volumes and a case, and a library was opened under the name of the "Association Library." The public were given the privileges of it by the payment of one dollar per annum for each person. The number of books was increased by donations and purchase until it reached about 150 volumes, and the selection was good. Issachar Shumway was first librarian. Changes were made in this office every three months. The books were kept for a time at the office, formerly Dr. Nichols', near the present Dr. Cushman house, since removed to Barton Street.

* Some of the entries on the records of fines are quite suggestive of the olden times, as when Mr. Lemuel Crane "greased Blackstone"; Peter Shumway "dropped tallow on the American Preacher"; Silas Eddy "dropped tallow on and burnt Stackhouse"; John Dana, "a drop of the candle on book"; Amos Shumway "blurred (snuff) Josephus." Fines for tallow drops were common.

In January, 1860, the interest in the Society had fallen off. In February, meetings were suspended and a committee chosen to care for the Library, funds, etc. In November, meetings were, by vote, discontinued.

The Library was removed to the store of B. W. Childs, one of the committee, and remained there for several years; and later the books were transferred to the Free Public Library.

HIGH SCHOOL.

The High School was opened in 1856. A year or two later a small library had been gathered for its use, chiefly by private contributions. In May, 1859, with a view to concentrate forces, the High School voted to incorporate its library with that of the Library Association, then in a flourishing condition. The books continued in the care of the Association for two years; and in May, 1861, at the closing up of its affairs, it was unanimously agreed to return to the school the volumes received, and also a case in which the whole had been kept, and the school library was re-established in its old position.

Additions to it have been made from time to time by private contributions, purchases from the proceeds of entertainments, etc., and the collection now numbers about 250 volumes,* and is considered a valuable adjunct to the educational appliances of the school.

* Since increased to upwards of 1500.

FARMERS' LIBRARY.

The Oxford Agricultural Library Association was formed July 25, 1859. The town had been canvassed by an agent of certain book publishers, and sixty-eight shares at three dollars each were sold. A constitution and by-laws were adopted, and a library of 148 volumes, costing $225, was established. George Hodges, Jr., was first president, and William E. Pease treasurer and librarian, continuing from first to last. The books were kept at the post-office, and for a few years were read; but, as few additions were made, interest declined, and on August 15, 1870, the collection was by unanimous vote given to the town to be incorporated in the Public Library.

SCHOOL LIBRARIES.

As early as 1841, school libraries were being printed and established in Massachusetts under the sanction of the Board of Education. The plan contemplated one hundred volumes, at a cost of $57. At this date thirty-seven volumes had been issued, and such a library was projected in District No. 7, North Gore, when $23.55 was raised by subscription and paid March 17, 1842. By-laws were adopted, officers chosen, and the library opened. In 1843 it became the property of the district. George W. Hartwell was chosen librarian, and the books were kept at his house.

By such enterprises, modest in their aims and pretensions, but suited to the wants of the times and communities in which they found birth, the way and no inconsiderable material were prepared for the Free Public Library. It owes its origin to the kindly regard and generous impulses of a distinguished son of the town, Hon. Ira M. Barton. Bearing in mind the benefits he, in his youth, received from a similar source, and the appreciation in which he had been held by the people, he gave in his will the sum of one thousand dollars towards establishing a Free Public Library.*

This gift was formally accepted by the town in April, 1868. In November, 1869, on the report of a committee appointed in April previous to consider the subject, it was voted to organize a town library under the provisions of the State laws. In April, 1870, it was voted to appropriate an ante-room of the High School house to its use, and a committee was chosen to fit up the same, purchase books, and provide for putting the library in operation, the expense of which was to be paid from the Barton Fund. The money refunded from the dog tax was appropriated to the library, in accordance with Chapter 250 of the Acts of 1869. In the autumn of 1870 the library was opened. In April, 1871, Charles A. Angell, George F. Daniels, and E. Har-

*Judge Barton's will, dated 1 June, 1867, contained the following: "One thousand dollars to the inhabitants of the Town of Oxford, my native place, towards establishing a Free Public Library in that town, as an inadequate return for the kindness and patronage of their fathers in my early professional life."

ris Howland were chosen a committee with the power to employ a librarian and to make by-laws. In 1874 the books, then numbering 1700, were removed to their present location in the Town Hall. The town has, since the beginning, with the exception of one or two years, voted to it the dog tax fund, which, besides paying current expenses, has increased the number of volumes to upwards of 4000.*

REFERENCE LIBRARY.

A most valuable feature of the Free Public Library is its Reference Department. It is rich in general works, art and other illustrated books, too cumbersome or too costly for the circulating department, but indispensable for occasional use. For this the town is indebted to the liberality of Hon. George L. Davis of North Andover, who, alive to the importance of public records and of proper indexes to make them available, in the spring of 1876 proposed to present to the town $500 for the benefit of its library, on condition that it would cause its earlier records of Births, Marriages, and Deaths to be copied and indexed. In April of the same year this offer was accepted, and the proposed work completed during the following summer.

The number of volumes in this department is about 450.†

In addition to the Circulating and Reference De-

---

* Now 8000.

† Now 1200.

partments, the Reading Table is constantly supplied with the following :—

Periodicals.*

MONTHLY.

North American Review.	*Forum.*
Harper's Magazine.	*Century.*
Scribner's.	*St. Nicholas.*
Cassell's Magazine of Art.	*Literary News.*
Traveler's Record.	*Manifesto.*

WEEKLY.

Illustrated London News.	*American Notes and*
Harper's Bazar.	*Queries.*
Youth's Companion.	*The Open Court.*
London Graphic.	*West Shore.*

* This list revised and brought up to date includes the following :—

QUARTERLY.

The Forum.

MONTHLY

The Atlantic.	*The North American Review.*
The Century.	*The Outing Magazine.*
The Cosmopolitan.	*The Outlook.*
Country Life in America.	*Public Libraries.*
Everybody's Magazine.	*The American Review of Reviews.*
Good Housekeeping.	*The School Arts Book.*
Harper's Bazar.	*Scribner's Magazine.*
Harper's Magazine.	*Success Magazine.*
Masters in Art.	*The Technical World.*
McClure's Magazine.	*The Protectionist.*
Munsey's Magazine.	*The Worcester Magazine.*
New England Magazine.	*The World's Work.*

WEEKLY.	JUVENILE.
Frank Leslie's.	*The American Boy.*
Harper's Weekly.	*Our Dumb Animals.*
The Illustrated London News.	*St. Nicholas.*
The Webster Times.	*The Youth's Companion.*
The Woman's Journal.	

With numerous occasional periodicals and other matter of current interest.

The rapid increase and growing appreciation of the Free Public Library are constantly impressing its larger demands and suggesting new devices for its improvement, and we cannot close this brief sketch more fittingly than by quoting from the Committee's last report the concluding paragraphs:

Provision for the future is a work requiring the co-operation of present and succeeding committees; of town authorities and their constituents; of all those who or whose ancestors have called Oxford their home; of public men who in the councils of state or nation have the disposal of public documents; of the wealthy and public-spirited, whether living or dying, and especially of our citizens, rich and poor alike, who by the exercise of generosity and self-denial can contribute an occasional book, picture or other object of interest, and, so, adding to the general aggregate, can engender and foster a feeling of individual proprietorship more helpful than wealth and its purchases.

In conclusion, it is proper to suggest another problem whose solution will fall to the not distant future, " What provision shall be made for this *protégé* of the town when it has outgrown its present quarters? " The good fortune of such towns as Concord, Quincy, Lincoln, Manchester-by-the-Sea, and a host of others whose public library buildings are at once a just cause of local pride and an honor to New England civilization, suggest the hope that some public-spirited benefactor may find immortality by linking his name to a modest architectural pile in which the Oxford Free Public Library may find its permanent home.

Ten years later this " Public-spirited Benefactor " whom the prophetic vision of a New England Faith dimly descried, appeared in the person of our esteemed former townsman, and the outcome is set forth in the last report of the Trustees of the Library.

EXTRACT

FROM THE

REPORT OF TRUSTEES,

1905.

In our annual report to the town last year, we were privileged to congratulate our fellow-citizens on the near completion of the magnificent new Library Building then in process of construction — the princely gift of Mr. CHARLES LARNED of Boston, a native and former resident of the town — for the use of the Free Public Library and as a perpetual memorial of his mother.

Since that report was made, the beautiful building has been finished, the extensive grounds have been graded, and the borders planted with a variegated selection of plants and shrubbery. The ancient elms at the front, the literal groves of great maples at the north and south, the massive edifice in the centre, and the tasteful walks and borders that conveniently span the boundaries, make the grounds, in the season of green leaf and blossom, one of the most charming spots in this or any other village.

And here we are happy to add one other fact to the above description. By deed of gift, signed,

CHARLES LARNED

in aid of the

CHARLES LARNED MEMORIAL

FIVE COURSES OF FREE LECTURES

1913, 19__ and 19__

Ten years later this "Public-spirited Benefactor" whom the prophetic vision of a New England Faith dimly descried, appeared in the person of our esteemed former townsman, and the outcome is set forth in the last report of the Trustees of the Library.

EXTRACT

FROM THE

REPORT OF TRUSTEES,

1905

In our annual report to the town last year, we were privileged to congratulate our fellow-citizens on the near completion of the magnificent new library building then in process of construction — the gift of Mr. CHARLES LARNED of Boston, native and former resident of the town — for the use of the Free Public Library and as a personal memorial of his mother.

Since that report was made, the beautiful building has been finished, the extensive grounds have been graded and the borders planted with a variety of trees and shrubbery. The an...... the massive edifice ...... borders ...... make the ...... blossom, ... ny other

...... feet to

...... signed,

sealed, and publicly delivered, all this has become the property of the town, and the town has entered into possession. Here, for all time, will be the home of the OXFORD FREE PUBLIC LIBRARY. Our limit is now about 8000 volumes. The building is planned to accommodate 40,000, so that we may safely say its conveniences will be ample for a hundred years to come, or so long as its massive walls shall withstand the dangers of fire and flood, or the slower disintegration of the elements.

It was in the spring of 1900, at the annual April meeting, that the purpose of Mr. Larned to donate a large sum toward a new library building was first made known to the town. The Library had outgrown its quarters in the rooms allotted to it in Memorial Hall, and its cramped and crowded condition had become a matter of serious consideration by the officials in charge and by the great public who availed themselves of its advantages. A readjustment of partitions to give more room would discommode other departments occupying the lower floor of the town building, and would be an expensive and, in the growing condition of the library, but a temporary remedy. The proposal of Mr. Larned, coming in this opportune time, was a practical solution of the difficult problem. The town accepted his generous offer with thanks, and chose a committee acceptable to Mr. Larned to select and purchase a site and to superintend the erection of the contemplated library building.

There was a delay of two years, during which a site was selected, plans procured, the contract given out, and everything made ready for the commencement of the work. It was at this stage that Mr. Larned assumed the whole financial responsibility. In the spring of 1903 ground was broken, the foundations put in, and during the season the work progressed toward completion. May 20 the corner stone was laid by the Most Worshipful Masonic Grand Lodge of Massachusetts, under the escort of the local Lodge. It was a magnificent ceremony, and the occasion was made a holiday in the town. In the winter and spring of 1904 the carpenters had finished their work, the elegant furniture was put in, the stack-rooms and book-shelves arranged, and, when all things were ready, the library was moved into its new home. On the 16th of July the doors were first opened to the public and the first books issued from the new quarters. The building had not then been given over to the town, and its early occupancy was therefore through the courtesy of the Building Committee.

But the 5th of October, 1904, was the great day in the history of the Library, when the title of this splendid property passed into the possession of the town, and the buildings and grounds dedicated by imposing ceremonials to the uses and purposes of the OXFORD FREE PUBLIC LIBRARY forever. These formalities took place in Memorial Hall, after an inspection of the new building and grounds by all who were interested. The house was packed with an audience composed of home-comers, former citizens, interested visitors, and our own people. Upon the platform were seated the town officers, the speakers, and the especial guests of the occasion, among whom was Mr. CHARLES LARNED, the observed of all observers as the generous giver of the building we were dedicating. The exercises, in brief, were as follows : —

INVOCATION . . . . Rev. I. A. Mesler

VOCAL MUSIC . . . . Double Quartet.

JOHN E. KIMBALL, Esq., Chairman of the Building Committee, presided, who, after an appropriate introductory address, called on the following gentlemen for brief responses : —

EDMUND M. BARTON, Librarian of the American Antiquarian Society and son of Hon. Ira M. Barton, the Founder of the Library.

SAMUEL S. GREEN, Librarian of the Free Public Library of Worcester.

Hon. DAVID I. ROBINSON, President of the Robinson Family Genealogical and Historical Association.

VOCAL MUSIC . . . . Oxford Male Quartet.

DELIVERY OF DEED AND KEYS to Town Authorities and transfer to Trustees of Library.

DEDICATORY PRAYER . . . . . Rev. Charles M. Carpenter

ADDRESS,

Hon. CARROLL D. WRIGHT, President of Clark College, Worcester.

SINGING, " AMERICA " . . The Audience, led by Quartet.

BENEDICTION . . . . Rev. Albert Tyler

The steps which have led to this consummation were as follows : —

At the Annual Town Meeting held on the 2 April, 1900, under Article 13,—" To see if the town will designate a Committee to confer with Mr. Charles Larned, of Boston, in relation to a proposed gift to the town," — the following letter was read by Mr. John E. Kimball : —

ROOM 1025, TREMONT BUILDING, BOSTON, MASS.,
February 15, 1900.

To THE VOTERS OF OXFORD :

Gentlemen, — It has been my desire, for many years, to do something in a substantial way for my native town where my parents lived and where their mortal remains repose.

If this desire is ever realized, it is important, not to say essential, that it should be, not only with the approval, but with the hearty co-operation, of the residents of the town.

My plan contemplates the erection of a building for the Free Public Library, which shall be a memorial to my mother. In designating the Free Public Library, I assume that there is no other institution in the town the promotion of whose interest would so enlist the sympathies of all the people. Also, aside from the promptings of filial gratitude, it seems to me not unfitting that we keep in remembrance those who, though best known in the domestic circle, trace their lineage to such Makers of New England as Rev. John Robinson, of Leyden.

I, therefore, respectfully suggest that, if deemed expedient, you provide for the selection of a Committee to confer with me at Boston in relation to the details of the project.

Respectfully yours,

CHARLES LARNED.

In accepting the proposition, it was unanimously

Resolved, That the voters of Oxford heartily respond to the suggestion of Mr. Charles Larned, of Boston, and in pursuance thereof designate as a

Committee for conference Messrs. Walter D. Tyler, Franklin G. Daniels, and Alfred M. Chaffee.

Resolved, That this Committee is instructed to communicate with Mr. Larned without delay, and hold itself in readiness to wait upon him at such time and place as he may indicate.

Resolved, That the result of this conference, the expenses of which shall be borne by the town, should be embodied in a written report to be submitted at a special meeting called by the Selectmen, as early as possible.

This special meeting was called for the evening of 29 May, 1900, at which the Committee made the following

REPORT.

The Committee appointed by the Town of Oxford at their annual meeting held April 2d, 1900, to confer with Mr. Charles Larned, of Boston, Mass., in relation to a proposed gift to the town, have completed their labors and offer the following report : —

The Committee waited upon Mr. Larned at his office in Boston on April 7th, and received the following proposition from him, viz : —

Mr. Larned wishes to cause to be erected in Oxford as a memorial to his mother a Free Public Library Building upon the following conditions : —

The building shall be used as a Free Public Library Building for all time, and to be always known as the " Charles Larned Memorial."

The cost of the building to be borne two-thirds by Mr. Larned and one-third by the town, and the cost to be from $15,000 to $18,000, exclusive of site.

The location to be central, with ample grounds, and the building to be set back from the street and the site to be acceptable to Mr. Larned, but to be provided by the town.

The building to be of brick or stone, and to be constructed in good workmanlike manner.

Your Committee, having talked with Mr. Larned concerning the best method of carrying out his ideas, offer, as a part of this report, the following resolution, viz. : —

Resolved, That the town accept the proposition of Mr. Larned, and that a committee of three citizens of Oxford, consisting of John E. Kimball, Orrin F. Joslin, and Alfred M. Chaffee, be hereby appointed a Building Committee.

It shall be the duty of this Committee to consider all practical locations for the building, to ascertain the cost of each and Mr. Larned's choice in the matter, and to report to the town at a special meeting to be called for that purpose, with their recommendations on the subject.

It shall be the duty of this Committee to attend to the erection of the building and all other matters appertaining to the subject.

> WALTER D. TYLER,
> ALFRED M. CHAFFEE, ⎫ *Committee.*
> FRANKLIN G. DANIELS, ⎭

Approved. CHARLES LARNED.

In the acceptance of this report it was voted to adopt the resolution incorporated therein, and that the Committee chosen report at an adjournment of this meeting to be held June 30 at 7.30 P.M.

A Committee of three, consisting of C. I. Rawson, C. S. Lyman, and H. A. Larned, was appointed by the Chair to wait upon Mr. O. F. Joslin, who had expressed his willingness to give a site for the building, for which a vote of thanks was passed at the adjourned meeting held on the 30 June, 1900.

In accordance with the above action the adjourned meeting was held at the date specified, and, the report of the Building Committee on a site for the Charles Larned Memorial being called for, it was presented by the Chairman as follows: —

To the Voters of Oxford:

In pursuance of instructions coupled with the appointment of a Building Committee at the special town meeting held on the 29 May, 1900, a careful and exhaustive examination of available locations for the proposed

Charles Larned Memorial

has been made in conjunction with Mr. Larned in person, and has resulted in reducing the question of selection to a choice between three eligible sites, to wit: the Hyde property, the White property, and the Cushman lot.

Aside from the essential features of ample space and central location, the considerations which have focussed the attention of your Committee upon these three sites are that all, perhaps in varying degrees, are easily accessible, reasonably quiet, adapted to proper architectural effect, upon the main street, upon the right side of the street, and well shaded.

The Hyde property, on the north-west corner of Main and Sigourney Streets, presents a frontage of about 180 feet on Main Street by 200 feet on Sigourney Street, and contains a two-story house with ells and barn. The price is $6,500.

The White property, near the Congregational church, consists of two lots,—a corner lot with a frontage of 109 feet on Main Street by 200 feet on Church Street, containing a dwelling and barn, also a lot of irregular form opposite the north-east corner of the old cemetery and contiguous to the first, with a frontage of 93 feet on Chureh Street, running north 133 feet, where it narrows to 40 feet, and containing a tenement house. All this property can be bought for $3,000 ; or a part of the corner lot, without the buildings, measuring 109 feet on Main Street and 109 feet on Church Street, for $1,500, on condition that the barn shall be moved a few feet to the west and made to front the east, at the town's expense.

The Cushman lot, immediately north of Mrs. Cushman's house, may be described as a parallelogram, with the north-east corner 42 feet front by 172 feet cut out: this leaves a frontage on Main Street of 88 feet, with a depth westward to the line of the High School lot of nearly 450 feet, and approaching within about 75 feet of Barton Street. The lot can be purchased for $1,200, and will cost the town nothing.

As other elements than mere eligibility of a site for library purposes enter into the problem of selection, it has seemed to your Committee to accord more fully with the spirit of the instructions given not to attempt to pronounce upon the question of cost by recommending unconditionally a specific site, but rather to eliminate non-essential features, and so reduce the problem to manageable proportions, and thus hand it over to the voters in the compact form which it now bears.

The considerations *pro* and *con* touching each of the above-named locations have been carefully canvassed by the Committee, but it has been thought best not to encumber this report by setting them forth in detail.

In view of the fact, however, that we are called upon to act, not for ourselves alone, but for generations yet unborn, and that probably no local question during all the years of the century now closing so vitally concerns the mental and moral well-being of the young people of Oxford, present and future, and while not unmindful of the limitations of our prerogatives as a committee appointed for a special purpose, it may not be improper to suggest that, as we have enjoyed and are now enjoying the bounty of a long line of liberal benefactors in the past, it becomes us, who are but temporary custodians of the welfare of others, to plan generously and well for the future Oxford in which we of to-day can be at best only a memory.

Respectfully submitted,

JOHN E. KIMBALL, } *Building*
ORRIN F. JOSLIN,   } *Committee.*
ALFRED M. CHAFFEE, }

OXFORD, MASS., 30 June, 1900.

A motion was then made by Mr. Lawrence F. Kilty, that " we reconsider the vote whereby we voted to accept the proposition offered by Mr. C. Larned, at a previous session of this meeting." Carried by a vote of 76 to 28, whereupon it was voted to lay the report of the Building Committee on the table.

Mr. Larned having in private generously intimated his willingness to allow his proposition of April, 1900, to remain open for action another year, which intimation was reaffirmed by a letter to the Committee dated at Cocoanut Grove, Fla., March

14, 1901, at the annual meeting held 1 April, 1901, the subject reappeared in Article 16 of the Warrant, — "To see if the town will accept the propositions of Mr. Charles Larned and Mr. Orrin F. Joslin in relation to a Free Public Library Building, and raise and appropriate money therefor, as petitioned for by John E. Kimball, Alfred M. Chaffee, and Orrin F. Joslin, or act thereon."

Mr. Joslin's proposition is embodied in the following memorandum: —

I propose to convey to the Town of Oxford by warranty deed all that portion of the present Cushman lot lying north of a line from a point on the Highway about 88 feet south of the Newton line, running westerly about 450 feet to the Barber line and including the section to the south and west of the Newton Estate, about 42 x 272 feet, upon the following conditions, viz. : —

The gift shall be held and occupied in perpetuity for a Free Public Library Building, or, if not all required for such building, the residue for a Free Public School Building. In case the Town prefers for such purpose some other site, I will give in lieu of the Cushman lot the sum of ($1,000) One Thousand Dollars.

ORRIN F. JOSLIN.
OXFORD, March 30, 1901.

It was voted to accept the propositions of Mr. Charles Larned and Mr. Orrin F. Joslin, and to carry into effect their provisions. The same Building Committee was appointed, and the sum of $500 was raised and appropriated for their expenses.

A special meeting of the voters was called for the

evening of 18 May, 1901, at which the following report was read and accepted : —

Your Committee, having discharged its duties, submit the following report : —

The Cushman Lot, about 88 feet front on Main Street and running back to the High School lot 1⅛ acres, will cost the town absolutely nothing.

The Cushman Farm, including the whole of the Cushman property, house and barn, between Mrs. Newton's and Mrs. Wheelock's, will cost the town $4,000.

The Morgan Corner, including it and the Chaffee property, two houses and one barn, will cost the town $4,900.

The Hyde Lot, house and barn, will cost the town $4,500.

The White Lot, north of the Congregational church, two houses and one barn, will cost the town $2,000.

The Sigourney Lot, 85 x 145 feet, opposite Town Hall, house and barn, will cost the town $3,000.

O. F. JOSLIN.
JOHN E. KIMBALL.
A. M. CHAFFEE.

From these the Hyde lot was selected by the following ballot : —

Whole number of votes cast, 152.

Blank	1
Sigourney Lot	1
White Lot	3
Cushman Farm	3
Cushman Lot	32
Morgan Lot	33
Hyde Lot	79

and the Building Committee was authorized to make the purchase.

It was then voted to sell the buildings, also to sell 80 feet of land fronting Sigourney Street, with the house and barn.

At a special meeting called for the evening of 17 September, 1901, after a nearly unanimous vote refusing to borrow and appropriate the sum of $4,500 for the purchase of the aforesaid Hyde lot it was

Voted, "To annul and revoke all acts and votes heretofore taken relative to a new building and site for a Library."

The way was thus cleared for history to repeat itself, and accordingly the Warrant for the next Annual Town Meeting held on the 7 April, 1902, contained such Articles as the following : —

Article 12.   To hear the report of the Library Building Committee and act thereon.

Article 13.   To see what action the town will take in regard to the gifts of Mr. Charles Larned and Mr. Orrin F. Joslin for a Free Public Library.

Article 14.   To raise and appropriate a sum of money not exceeding Fifty-seven Hundred Dollars ($5700) to pay for the Hyde Lot as purchased by the Building Committee, as authorized by vote of the town at a Special Town Meeting held May 18, 1901.

Article 15.   To raise and appropriate the sum of Eighteen Hundred Dollars ($1800) to build a Free Public Library, or act thereon etc.

The outcome was a new departure in the passage of two motions, both by Mr. Edwin Bartlett:—

That the School Committee act in conjunction with the old Library Committee (*sic*), and confer with Mr. Charles Larned in relation to a Library and High School Building combined, and report at a special meeting to be called as soon as possible.

also

To authorize the Library Committee, J. E. Kimball, O. F. Joslin, A. M. Chaffee, and the School Committee, acting jointly, to propose to Mr. Larned to allow his gift of $12,000 and accrued interest to be used in building a Union Building to contain a library and the high school, costing not to exceed $28,000.

At the special meeting called for the evening of 6 May, 1902, "to hear the report of the joint Committee in regard to a Union Building to accommodate a High School and a Library," the report was as follows:—

OXFORD, MASS., May 6, 1902.

Your joint Committee appointed at our last Annual Town Meeting to confer with Mr. Charles Larned in regard to using his gift and accrued interest in the construction of a Union Building to accommodate a Library and High School, having discharged its duty, submit the following

REPORT.

On Saturday, April 12, Edwin N. Bartlett, David Glass, O. F. Joslin, and A. M. Chaffee, went to Boston on the 8.58 train from Worcester, going direct to the office of Mr. Larned.

After a careful consideration of the subject Mr.

Larned signified his willingness to write a letter setting forth his views, which letter reads as follows : —

Mr. A. M. CHAFFEE,
Oxford, Mass.

Dear Sir, — Replying to your request that I write you a letter defining my position on a proposed building for library and school combined, I beg leave to say that a combination building for library and school for the town of Oxford has to my mind many serious objections; but, should the voters of Oxford decide that a combination building is what they want, my offer of $12,000, with interest thereon, I am willing should be used as part payment for such a building, which you tell me may cost about $28,000.

The Building Committee to remain as named in my original proposition.

Trusting that herein I have covered all the points of your inquiry, I remain,

Very truly yours,

CHARLES LARNED.

On Monday, April 14th, your joint Committee met at the residence of Mr. O. F. Joslin to discuss the matter, and after careful consideration of the subject it was decided that your Committee make no recommendations, but desire that the voters should carefully consider the propositions and decide the question as it seems in their wisdom best.

On April 18th your Committee received a further communication from Mr. Larned, as follows : —

BOSTON, MASS., April 18, 1902.

Mr. A. M. CHAFFEE,
Oxford, Mass.

Dear Sir, — You doubtless have my letter of April 15. I would like to say in addition that, should the town vote to build a library building on the Hyde lot and a school building on another lot, I would be pleased to donate $1,000 toward the school building. In that case the town would have full control of erection of school building.

Yours truly,

CHARLES LARNED.

In conclusion the Committee would recommend that, whatever action the town may take in the premises, that a vote of thanks be passed expressive of their appreciation of Mr. Charles Larned's and Mr. O. F. Joslin's most generous offers.

All of which is most respectfully submitted,

O. F. JOSLIN.
A. M. CHAFFEE.
JOHN E. KIMBALL.
DAVID GLASS.
JOHNSON R. WOODWARD.
EDWIN N. BARTLETT.

It was voted to accept the report of the joint Committee, including the two letters from Mr. Charles Larned, and that the same be spread upon the records of the town.

At this meeting it was also voted that the Selectmen and Treasurer be directed to borrow a sum not to exceed Fifty-seven Hundred Dollars ($5700) to pay for the Hyde lot, purchased by the Building

Committee, as authorized by vote of the town at a Special Town Meeting held 18 May, 1901.

Under another article, that they be directed to turn over the license fees for this year to the Library Building Committee.

(This "*tainted money*" was subsequently turned back into the treasury.)

And, finally, "that the town accept the gifts of Mr. Charles Larned and Mr. Orrin F. Joslin in relation to a Free Public Library,—said gifts, Twelve Thousand Dollars ($12,000), with interest, from Mr. Larned, and One Thousand Dollars ($1,000) from Mr. Joslin, coupled with conditions which they have stated in writing,"—with a vote of thanks to these gentlemen, with acceptance, thanks, and acknowledgment for Mr. Larned's gift of One Thousand Dollars ($1,000) for a High School Building.

In the accepted belief that, despite the contradictions of two years' experience the final vote of acceptance meant what it purported to mean, the policy of obstruction seeming to have fairly exhausted itself, from this time the enterprise progressed steadily and without interruption to its final accomplishment. Henceforth the Building Committee was left to prosecute its work unmolested, and at the Annual Town Meeting held on 6 April, 1903, reported progress as follows :—

Perhaps no report from this Committee is called for till our work is done. When that period arrives, we hope the work will speak for itself. Conscious of the fact, however, that the public is deeply interested, we have deemed it best to report progress coupled with some considerations touching its financial aspect.

One year ago, as you remember, preliminary sketches by several architects were submitted, which led to the choice of Cutting, Carlton & Cutting of Worcester, who proceeded at once to embody our plan in working drawings. On the completion of plan and specifications the season was too far advanced to justify an attempt to erect the building before winter. The time was improved, however, in devising improvements in the plan, selecting materials, and seeking out the right men. The contract was finally, in January, awarded to Rankin & Woodside of Worcester, for the sum of $21,100 and the stone and brick on the lot. Meanwhile the buildings and other property had been sold and removed, and the site placed in readiness for the builders, who began work about two weeks ago.

It will be remembered that a printed statement submitted to the town in 1902 represented the "Balance" over and above available funds "needed to complete the library building" to be $1,800, the members of the Building Committee being personally pledged to be responsible for any excess in cost over $18,000.

A letter just received from Mr. Larned may modify these conditions by relieving the town of the necessity of raising even the $1,800, and placing at our disposal for better and more complete equipment the funds already on deposit.

The letter is as follows:—

ROOM 1025 TREMONT BUILDING, BOSTON, MASS.,
April 3, 1903.

To THE VOTERS OF OXFORD:

Gentlemen,—Whereas the town has generously secured and purchased a more expensive and eli-

37

gible lot for the Free Public Library building than was at first anticipated, said lot being devoted exclusively to the library building, and on which said building is now in process of erection, and whereas said library building will, when completed, cost largely in excess of the original sum mentioned, $18,000, after due consideration I have decided, with the consent and approval of the town, to modify my original proposition, to wit : —

To assume and bear the entire expense and cost of the library building up to the sum of Twenty-four Thousand Dollars ($24,000), thereby enabling the town, through the Building Committee, to furnish and equip the library in a more liberal manner than they would otherwise feel like doing.

Very truly yours,

CHARLES LARNED.

Perhaps the Building Committee might consider its duty p discharged when the building was completed, and leave the matter of equipment and adornment of grounds to other hands; but the comprehensive plan upon which we have labored covers every detail inside and outside the building, all of which should be harmoniously wrought out, and it would be more in accordance with the fitness of things, not to sa our own views, to turn over the property finishedy equipped, and ready for use.

Therefore, we submit the following recommendations :—

I. That the proposition embodied in the accompanying letter of Mr. Charles Larned be accepted with appropriate acknowledgments.

II. That the proceeds of the sale of buildings and other property on the library premises be appropriated to the grading and laying out of the grounds.

III.   That all funds in the town treasury or on deposit available for library purposes be turned over to the Building Committee, to be used, or such portion thereof as may be necessary, to properly furnish and equip the new building.

JOHN E. KIMBALL,
O. F. JOSLIN,
A. M. CHAFFEE,
} *Building Committee of the Charles Larned Memorial.*

OXFORD, MASS., 6 April, 1903.

The report was supplemented by the statement that the property on the Hyde lot had been sold for nearly $700, and that the Building Committee this day had voted to refund to the town the $2,250 license money set apart for their use on 6 May, 1902.

By a unanimous vote the report of the Building Committee was adopted, and thanks tendered to Mr. Charles Larned, of Boston, for his generous additional gift, which the Town Clerk was instructed to enter upon the records and communicate to Mr. Larned.

At the Annual Town Meeting held on 3 April, 1905, after the completion and dedication of the building, the following resolutions were unanimously adopted : —

Resolved, That the inhabitants of the Town of Oxford desire to place upon record an expression of their appreciation and gratitude for the munificent gift of the recently dedicated to the use of the Free Public Library.

It will stand through the years to come a monument of rare public spirit guided by wisdom and intelligent foresight, while presenting to old and young an ever-abiding object-lesson inspiring loyalty and filial gratitude and beckoning to higher planes of thought and life.

While thus voicing the sentiment of every resident of Oxford, coupled with the hope that the generous Donor may long be spared to witness and enjoy the fruits of his noble benefaction, we trust he may find satisfaction and reward in the reflection that such acts are not bounded by the span of a single life, but are self-perpetuating and immortal.

Resolved, That the claim upon Mr. Charles Larned for $1,000, pledged for a High School Building to forestall the adoption of a plan whose unwisdom is now universally recognized, is hereby voluntarily relinquished.

LAYING OF THE CORNER-STONE.

Excavation having been made and the foundations completed, the 20 May, 1903, was designated for the ceremony of Laying the Corner-stone. An invitation had been extended to the Masonic Grand Lodge of Massachusetts to take charge of this ceremonial, whose acceptance and willing service were highly appreciated by the citizens and invited guests. Weather conditions were most favorable, and when at 2.30 P.M. the representatives of the Grand Lodge, consisting of Most Worshipful Grand Master Baalis Sanford and fifteen associates, escorted by the local lodge and led by the Pulaski Cornet Band of Webster, reached the site of the building, they were welcomed by a concourse whose number and enthusiasm were in keeping with the significance of the occasion.

The exercises were opened by the following hymn sung by the Worcester Masonic Quartet : —

> Great Architect of earth and heaven,
>   By time nor space confined,
> Enlarge our love to comprehend
>   Our brethren, all mankind.
>
> Where'er we are, whate'er we do,
>   Thy presence let us own ;
> Thine eye, all-seeing, marks our deeds,
>   To Thee all thoughts are known,

While Nature's works and Science's laws
    We labor to reveal,
Oh! be our duty done to Thee
    With fervency and zeal.

With FAITH our guide, and humble HOPE,
    Warm CHARITY and LOVE,
May all, at last, be raised to share
    Thy perfect light above.

The formal request for the service of the order was extended by the Chairman of the Building Committee in these words:

Most Worshipful Grand Master, Guests and Friends:

A former resident of this historic town, actuated by a sentiment of filial gratitude and regard for the well-being of the people of his early home, is erecting upon this spot a permanent abode for an institution which is typical of New England community life in the twentieth century.

It means much to us, it is even more significant to the nation, the corner-stone of whose fabric rests upon the intelligence of the masses and whose institutions open up the avenues of wealth to the private citizen, native and foreign born alike, at the same time prompting the consecration of wealth to noblest uses.

We are here to-day publicly to inaugurate the enterprise so auspiciously begun; and in recognition of your ancient and honorable order, whose traditions are linked with some of the most notable structures of the Old and New Worlds, past and present, we have invited you, sir, and your associates, as representatives of that order, to come hither and, in the presence of an appreciative public in whose interest the work is done, to officiate, according to established forms, in laying the corner-stone of the

CHARLES LARNED MEMORIAL,

the permanent home of the

FREE PUBLIC LIBRARY OF OXFORD.

The response of the Grand Master was as follows:

Mr. Chairman and Brethren:

From time immemorial it has been the custom of the Ancient and Honorable Fraternity of Free and Accepted Masons, when requested so to do, to lay, with ancient forms, the corner-stones of buildings, both public and private, devoted to learning, to benevolence, to religion, and for the purposes of the administration of justice and free government and the commemoration of great and humane benefactions to mankind.

And we are assembled here to-day to lay this corner-stone in accordance with our law; and thus renewedly testifying our reverence and love for Him whom we worship as the Giver and Guardian of our souls, and our respect, loyalty, and allegiance to the laws of our country, we shall proceed in accordance with ancient usage.

Let us first give our attention to the contemplation of a lesson from the "Book of the Law," and in accordance with the usual Masonic custom at the commencement of every undertaking unite with our Reverend Grand Chaplain in an invocation to the Great Architect of worlds, that his mercy and favor may be with us, and with the whole brotherhood of man.

The following selections with responses by the brethren were then read by Rev. Albert Tyler, Chaplain of the Oxford Lodge : —

CHAPLAIN. Bless the Lord, O my soul. O Lord my God, thou art very great; thou art clothed with honor and majesty. *Psalm* civ. 1.

BRETHREN. But thou, O Lord, shalt endure for ever; and thy remembrance unto all generations. *Psalm* cii. 12.

CHAPLAIN. Thou shalt arise, and have mercy upon Zion : for the time to favor her, yea, the set time, is come. *Psalm* cii. 13.

BRETHREN. For thy servants take pleasure in her stones, and favor the dust thereof. *Psalm* cii. 14.

CHAPLAIN. Where wast thou when I laid the foundations of the earth? declare, if thou hast understanding. *Job* xxxviii. 4.

BRETHREN. Who hath laid the measures thereof, if thou knowest? or who hath stretched the line upon it? *Job* xxxviii. 5.

CHAPLAIN. Whereupon are the foundations thereof fastened? or who laid the corner-stone thereof? *Job* xxxviii. 6.

BRETHREN. When the morning stars sang together, and all the sons of God shouted for joy? *Job* xxxviii. 7.

CHAPLAIN. Is it time for you, O ye, to dwell in your ceiled houses, and this house lie waste? Thus saith the Lord of hosts : Go up to the mountain, and bring wood, and build the house; and I will take pleasure in it, and I will be glorified, saith the Lord. *Haggai* i. 4, 7, 8.

BRETHREN. Ye also, as lively stones, are built up a spiritual house, an holy priesthood, to offer up spiritual sacrifices acceptable to God. 1 *Peter* ii. 5.

CHAPLAIN. Therefore thus saith the Lord God, Behold, I lay in Zion for a foundation a stone, a tried stone, a precious corner-stone, a sure foundation : he that believeth shall not make haste. Judgment also will I lay to the line and righteousness to the plummet. *Isaiah* xxviii. 16, 17.

BRETHREN. Open to me the gates of righteousness : I will go into them, and I will praise the Lord. *Psalm* cxviii. 19.

Honor and majesty are before him, strength and beauty are in his sanctuary. *Psalm* xcvi. 6.

CHAPLAIN. Except the Lord build the house, they labor in vain that build it : except the Lord keep the city, the watchman waketh but in vain. *Psalm* cxxvii. 1.

BRETHREN. One generation shall praise thy works to another, and shall declare thy mighty acts. They shall abundantly utter the memory of thy great goodness, and shall sing of thy righteousness. *Psalm* cxlv. 4, 7.

CHAPLAIN. O come, let us worship and bow down : let us kneel before the Lord our Maker. *Psalm* xcv. 6.

BRETHREN. For he is our God ; and we are the people of his pasture, and the sheep of his hand. *Psalm* xcv. 7.

CHAPLAIN. Sing unto the Lord, bless his name ;

show forth his salvation from day to day. *Psalm* xcvi. 2.

BRETHREN. All thy works shall praise thee, O Lord; and thy saints shall bless thee. *Psalm* cxlv. 10.

Yea, they shall sing in the ways of the Lord: for great is the glory of the Lord. *Psalm* cxxxviii. 5.

Prayer was offered by the Grand Chaplain, Rev. Charles A. Skinner, after which a list of articles deposited in the copper receptacle enclosed in the corner-stone was read by the Grand Treasurer, Henry G. Fay, as follows: —

1. Documentary History of the Charles Larned Memorial.
2. Sealed Package from Mr. Larned, the Donor of the Building.
3. A Copy of the Town Report for 1890, containing a History of the Free Public Library.
4. Catalogue of the Free Public Library — 1895.
5. Daniels' "History of Oxford."
6. Freeland's "Records of Oxford."
7. The Assessors' Report for 1902.
8. Town Report for 1903, with the Present Board of Selectmen and the Building Committee.
9. Oxford and Auburn Directory — 1903.
10. Copy of *The Mid-Weekly* for Wednesday, 11 August, 1897.
11. History of Masonry in Oxford from 1795 to 1903.
12. Collection of Forty or Fifty Photographs and Local Views in Oxford, including a View of the Foundations of this Building.
13. Miscellaneous Local Documents, Business Cards, etc.
14. The McKinley Memorial.
15. Copies of the *St. Louis Globe-Democrat* and the *St. Louis Republic*, containing an account of the Inauguration Ceremonies of "The Louisiana Purchase Exposition."

16. A Set of Silver and Minor Proof Coins for 1903, from the United States Mint at Philadelphia, Pa.

17. Specimens of Fractional Currency issued during the War of the Rebellion.

18. Copies of *The Worcester Telegram* and *The Worcester Spy* for 20 May, 1903.

The corner-stone in place, the imposing ritual was continued by the Application of the Jewels, the Libation of Corn by the Deputy Grand Master, J. Gilman Waite, —

> When once of old in Israel,
>   Our earthly brethren wrought with toil,
> Jehovah's blessing on them fell
>   In showers of Corn, and Wine, and Oil.—

the Libation of Wine by the Senior Grand Warden, John A. McKim, —

> When there a shrine to Him alone
>   They built, with worship, sin to foil,
> On threshold and on corner-stone,
>   They poured out Corn, and Wine, and Oil.—

the Libation of Oil by the Junior Grand Warden, William H. H. Soule, —

> And we have come, fraternal bands,
>   With joy and pride, and prosperous spoil,
> To honor Him by votive hands
>   With streams of Corn, and Wine, and Oil.—

an Invocation by the Grand Chaplain, the Presentation of Working Tools to the Architect, and the closing address by the Grand Master : —

May this undertaking be conducted and completed by the craftsmen according to the grand plan in Peace, Harmony, and Brotherly Love; and by the skill and taste of the architect may an edifice here arise which shall render new service and honor to this ancient town.

May it be blessed with Wisdom in the plan, Strength in the execution, Beauty in the adornment; and may the Sun of Righteousness enlighten those who build, the generous Donor, and the community for whose benefit this structure shall be erected.

Proclamation was duly made by the Grand Marshal Frank W. Mead, and after the singing of the hymn, —

> Lord! Thou hast been our dwelling-place,
>   Through years of old and ages past;
> And still Thy laws we seek to trace.
>   On Thee our trust we humbly cast,
> Father of Light!   Builder Divine!
>   Behold our work, and make it Thine,—

the address of the day was delivered by Rev. William H. Rider, D.D., of Gloucester, Mass.

As this address by force of circumstances was largely *impromptu*, it cannot be reproduced, but was listened to with close attention and deep interest.

The flowering beauty of the opening spring-time suggested to the speaker the more beautiful sentiment of maternal and filial love from which emanated this project and this occasion. By a natural transition it was declared most fitting that a fraternity seeking light and "More Light," thus leading to the Source of all knowledge, should participate in the consecration of a building sacred to tender memories and all best thought and life.

Familiar as is the dedication of libraries in New England, we shall never see too many of them.

The victories of the twentieth century are to be intellectual, victories of science and education. The war-drums are muffled, and a new song, the song of peace and good will to men, is heard in the land. The prophecy of this peace is to be fulfilled by just such buildings as this.

There is nothing to be compared with the lasting effects of a public library in a community. It is the privilege of everybody in such community to keep company with the ages.

Not one of all the marvelous things that have come to us through modern improvements—the trolley car, the electric light, the telephone, the telegraph—is to be compared in real value to a good book. It transformed Abraham Lincoln from an ignorant boy into the First American.

Books are light-houses erected in the great sea of time. He who gives, gives also guides for finest conduct and inspires with greatest hope.

In conclusion, the speaker made among other practical suggestions this excellent recommendation, that the library which was to be here installed should be made complete in some one line, be it a department of history, of science, or of literature, so that it should be known far and wide as possessing an exceptionally rich, if not exhaustive, collection in that special department.

The singing of " America " by the assemblage

and the benediction pronounced by the Grand Chaplain concluded the exercises of a day memorable in the history of the town.

In response to the following invitation, at the hour appointed the auditorium of Memorial Hall was filled with an expectant assemblage made up of present and former residents of Oxford, invited guests from all parts of Massachusetts and neighboring States, including names prominent in literary, professional, and public life.

Oxford, Massachusetts.

will take place in Said Hall

Memorial Hall

5 October ... at 1:30 o'clock p. m.

by Hon. Carroll D. Wright.

your presence is respectfully requested.

Holland

John E. Kimball
Orrin F. Joslin   } Building
Alfred M. Chaffee } Committee.

51

MARRIED

29 April, 1817, Jonas Learned, of Oxford, M

DIED

4 May, Jonas the Children of Josephus

DESCENDED

through

arles, Elijah, Benjamin, Peter, I

, from

Rev. John Robinson, of eyden

Holland

DEDICATION.

The

Dedication

of the

Charles Larned Memorial

— In memory of Clarissa Robinson Larned —

to the use of the

Free Public Library

Oxford, Massachusetts,

will take place at

Memorial Hall

on Wednesday, 5 October, 1904, at 1:30 o'clock p. m.

Address by Hon. Carroll D. Wright.

The honor of your presence is respectfully requested.

John E. Kimball ⎫
Orrin F. Joslin ⎬ Building
Alfred M. Chaffee ⎭ Committee.

Dedication
Program.
5 October, 1904.

Invocation.

VOCAL MUSIC, "Jehovah Reigns."   *Mendelssohn.*

DOUBLE QUARTET.

Introductory.

Responses.

"HON. IRA M. BARTON, Founder of the Free Public Library."

EDMUND M. BARTON, American Antiquarian Society.

"PUBLIC LIBRARIES IN MASSACHUSETTS."

C. B. TILLINGHAST, Chairman of Free Public Library Commission of Massachusetts.

"THE PUBLIC LIBRARY AS A PUBLIC EDUCATOR."

SAMUEL S. GREEN, Free Public Library of Worcester.

"THE ROBINSON FAMILY."

HON. DAVID I. ROBINSON, President of the Robinson Family Genealogical and Historical Association.

VOCAL MUSIC, "The Old Arm-chair," *Eliza Cook, music by Henry Russell.*

OXFORD MALE QUARTET.

Delivery of Deed and Keys

TO TOWN AUTHORITIES — TO TRUSTEES OF LIBRARY.

Dedicatory Prayer.

REV. CHARLES M. CARPENTER.

Address.

HON. CARROLL D. WRIGHT.

SINGING, "America."

The AUDIENCE, led by the QUARTET.

Benediction.

52

The exercises conformed to the above program, John E. Kimball, Esq., Chairman of the Building Committee presiding.

CHAIRMAN: The divine blessing will be invoked by Rev. I. A. Mesler, of Oxford.

INVOCATION.

We are very grateful, our Heavenly Father, for that which brings us together to-day. We recognize the fact that every good gift and every perfect gift cometh from thee. We pray for thy blessing upon it. We pray for thy blessing upon all the exercises of this day. May the Holy Spirit rest upon those who shall speak to us, and guide in every thought and every word! In Jesus' name we ask it. Amen.

SINGING.

Jehovah Reigns.

CHAIRMAN:

Ladies and Gentlemen,— In behalf of the Building Committee of the Charles Larned Memorial I extend to you a cordial welcome and thanks for the interest manifested by your presence. There are scores, perhaps hundreds, who would like to be here, but cannot, and I am constrained to read, in their behalf, a sample letter of regret expressive of the sentiments of those who, from age or infirmity, distance, or other engagements can be with us to-day only in spirit : —

I am **very grateful** for the invitation so kindly **sent me the 25th to attend** the exercises in Memorial Hall October 5, and **regret** that I cannot be present at that time. Certainly, my native town is **to be congratulated** that the generosity of her public-spirited son— **Mr. Charles Larned** — has taken such a **beautiful** form, one which not only adds attraction to her main street, but which will furnish her **residents** pleasure and profit so long as the memorial shall stand. May it be a " joy forever!"

It was a happy thought of Mr. Larned to associate his mother's name with the building, and I trust this silent witness of a son's filial love and respect will be a lesson to all the young people who **frequent** the Library, and be an aid in making them **also** noble sons and daughters.

Friends, we have met to dedicate to public uses a building typical of what is best in New England civilization,— filial reverence and gratitude, intelligence and character in the masses, and public spirit, which is but another name for patriotism.

It is not for us to know what tender memories and cherished associations are built into this memorial temple, imparting a touch of peculiar grace to this happy combination of utility and beauty. That belongs to the sacred privacy of the domestic circle, which we may not invade; but we do know the value of such sentiments in molding character and shaping destiny, not alone of individuals, but of nations; we do know that loyalty in the home begets loyalty to the State, the logical outcome of which is individual and social betterment.

This simple ceremonial may fade from the memory and be forgotten; methods and usages will change, grow old, and be superseded by that which is better, but the lessons of yonder structure will deepen with the years, they can never become obsolete, for they are vital to our continuance as a people, and, happily, in their very nature are self-perpetuating.

The conditions which render this gift timely and most acceptable are the growth of more than a generation. A flourishing Free Public Library has long been the *protégé* and pride of the people. Oxford has been fortunate in her benefactors! We congratulate the recipients of Mr. Carnegie's bounty, and all honor to that broad philanthropy which has given us a new lesson in the uses of great wealth, while doing so much to cement the brotherhood of the nations! But we count ourselves more fortunate. Our benefactors are "to the manner born" and bred among us, and their benefactions are evidence not only of successful endeavor and generous impulses, but of affection and gratitude as well. Especially is this true of the honored Founder of our Free Public Library, who in his will remembered the inhabitants of his native town by a gift for that purpose " *as an inadequate return for the kindness and patronage of their Fathers,*" and it will be a special pleasure to hear a word from the representative of Hon. Ira M. Barton in the person of his son, Edmund M. Barton, of Worcester.

Mr. BARTON:

Mr. Chairman,—My duty is strictly filial, it seems to me, to-day. On beautiful Oxford plain there were born into the family of which my honored father was the head four sons and one daughter; while Worcester was the birthplace of three sons and one daughter. Among the papers of the first-born—William Sumner Barton, born in Oxford, Sept. 30, 1824—is a brief sketch of the founder of this library, to which I call your attention during the few moments allowed me.

The Hon. Ira Moore Barton, of Worcester, first named Ira, was born in Oxford, Oct. 25, 1796, and in 1839, by act of the General Court, was authorized to take the additional name of Moore in memory of his revered maternal grandmother, Dorothy Moore, and of his great-great-grandfather Moore, the first magistrate of his native town. He was a grandson of Dr. Stephen Barton, who was born at Sutton, June 10, 1740. Dr. Barton's father and mother, Edmund and Anna Flynt Barton, were married in Salem, April 9, 1739, and probably moved to Sutton soon afterward. Mr. Barton graduated with high honors at Brown University in 1819, and at the Cambridge Law School in 1822. He practised law in Oxford from 1822 to 1834, and was representative from that town during the years 1830 to 1832, inclusive. In 1833–34 he represented the county of Worcester in the State Senate. He removed to Worcester in 1834, and in 1836 was appointed by Governor Everett judge of probate for Worcester County. In 1840 he was chosen one of the electors for President in the famous Harrison or log-cabin campaign. He resigned his judgeship in 1844, and in 1846 represented the then town of Worcester in the legislature. Judge Barton continued the practice of his profession until 1849, when he visited Europe in pursuit of much-needed rest and recreation. Upon his return in 1850 he resumed his office practice only, finding leisure during the intervals of business for the indulgence of his literary, historical, and antiquarian tastes. He was an active member and for many years a councilor of the American Antiquarian Society. He died very suddenly at his home in Worcester, July 18, 1867.

I submit also the following character picture by one who knew him intimately: "Judge Barton was distinguished for purity, simplicity, and integrity of character; and as a public servant, in numerous offices of trust and responsibility, his conduct was marked by signal ability, fidelity, and success. He was eminently the accomplished lawyer, the upright magistrate, the enlightened patriotic citizen; and the community which, through a long and busy life, he has benefited and honored, will hold in grateful remembrance his services and his virtues. He has been described as a man of very striking personal appearance, with tall and commanding figure, fine head and Websterian eyes. He showed something of the Roman mould in his aspect, which was well reflected in his character."

The tributes paid by Mr. George F. Daniels in his History of Oxford and by Samuel Foster Haven, LL.D., in his Report of the Council of the American

· Antiquarian Society, read Oct. 21, 1867, may well be had in remembrance.

While this beautiful memorial appeals strongly to the gratitude of all, the surviving children of the founder may lay claim to a special cause for thankfulness to the wise and generous giver.

CHAIRMAN : The Free Public Library Commission has achieved an enviable reputation in placing Massachusetts in the forefront of States on either side of the Atlantic in free library facilities for the people. We hoped to listen to its chairman to-day, but instead the following letter comes to hand this morning : —

FREE PUBLIC LIBRARY COMMISSION

OF

MASSACHUSETTS.

Oct. 4, 1904.

JOHN E. KIMBALL, Esq., Chairman, etc. :

My dear Mr. Kimball,— Though it will be impracticable for me to accept your kind invitation to participate in the dedicatory services of the Charles Larned Memorial, I wish to express through you my appreciation of the gift which has come to your people and which enriches the Commonwealth.

I have known something of the sweet spirit the giver has shown in his desire to provide a building which shall be a source of inspiration and pride to the present and future citizens of his native town.

Similar gifts are not uncommon in Massachusetts. They bear witness to the growing sentiment that the library, supplementing the public school, adds to the pleasures and refinement of the home, the happiness and prosperity of the people, and the civic virtues which insure good citizenship and pure government.

All honor to Mr. Larned, a modest and philanthropic citizen, who, from the results of a lifetime of mercantile honor and thrift, provides a chaste, beautiful, and permanent home for the literary treasures that tend to perpetuate and increase the wisdom and intelligence which are the heritage of New England culture.

Yours most cordially,

C. B. TILLINGHAST,

Chairman,
Free Public Library Commission.

Fortunately, however, we have another representative of the Commission in our neighbor of the Free Public Library of Worcester.   He can tell us all about Libraries and the Library Commission, for, wherever they are in evidence, we are quite sure to see or hear the name of, Samuel S. Green.

MR. GREEN :

Mr. President, Ladies and Gentlemen,—It is my first duty and my pleasure to greet you in behalf of the libraries of the Commonwealth.   In 1890, when the Free Public Library Commission was established, the record of Massachusetts had been most honorable when compared with that of any other State.   But still there were one hundred and three towns which at that time had no public library.   I am able to say to you to-day that there is not remaining in this State a single town that has not a public library. All these towns sympathize with you to-day as you come here to dedicate this beautiful and convenient building, for which you are indebted to the munificence of the venerable gentleman who sits here upon the platform. In the name of the Public Library Commission of the Commonwealth, in behalf of the libraries of this State, in behalf of its whole people, I thank him for what Mr. Tillinghast says he has done,— "enriching the Commonwealth."

I must also greet you, ladies and gentlemen, in behalf of the library of the principal town in this county. Please accept of the hospitalities of the Free Public Library of Worcester, and I will add with Mr. Barton, the librarian, and Colonel Wright, a member of the Council, that I also, as a member of the Council, extend to you a cordial welcome to use the library of the American Antiquarian Society.

You have asked me, Mr. President, to speak upon public libraries as educational institutions. It is not only in their connections with colleges and schools that libraries exert an educational influence. I suppose, when I speak of them as instruments of value in connection with formal educational institutions, you wish me to speak mainly of their usefulness to the public schools, even though this town has the name of one of the great universities of the world. But a word before I do this. This is a town of farms. Is it not true that the best farmers here are those who attend institutes, read agricultural papers, and make themselves conversant with agricultural literature? What are you doing when you do this thing? Why, you are simply educating yourselves by adding to your own experience as farmers and to the results of experience which has been given to you by your fathers and neighbors the experience of other men engaged in similar pursuits as recorded in books,—the experience often of men who have had rare opportunities for experiment and investigation, and the results of whose researches it is of the greatest value for you to become acquainted with. What an educational influence, then, Mr. President, may a library exert in a town if the farmers of the town read papers and magazines, United States and Massachusetts Agricultural Reports, and books treating of the various departments of agriculture! What a blessing a library may be if the people use this kind of books, and if they are provided for them in sufficient numbers in the town!

There is manufacturing in Oxford. Suppose for an instant that everybody connected with a large shop—the proprietor, the manager, the foreman, and the workmen—were all readers; suppose they made it, all of them, their business to become acquainted with the principles of science which underlie the processes which they are engaged in performing every day; supposing they paid especial attention to the literature of the particular occupation in which they are engaged,—can you doubt for an instant that the products of that shop would be better or that instructed managers and informed workmen would do better work, that there would be more inventions, and that the value of the work of all would be so much increased that higher wages and salaries would be commanded?

But, Mr. President, I suppose that you wish me to speak especially of the connection of libraries with public schools. Supposing a library affords especial privileges to teachers, allows them to take a considerable number of books which they may need in preparing themselves for school exercises ; supposing the teacher is allowed to take a still larger number of books to be used in any way he pleases for the benefit of the scholars—do you not see at once that those teachers and scholars have a great advantage over such as do not have such privileges? How much more interesting and profitable a teacher can make his work if he can have accessible a large library of books, and be able to take to the school-room and to his home a considerable number to use in connection with the work in hand ! How much more interesting it is to a scholar to be allowed, when he is studying upon any subject, to read graphic and interesting accounts of that subject to add to the interest which comes from a dry paragraph in a text-book alluding to the subject ! Why, ladies and gentlemen, you can often make study fascinating to children if you point out to them sources of information where, in an interesting way and with a profusion of details, matters treated of briefly in their text-books are treated of at length and in a clear and agreeable style in larger books accessible to them in public libraries.

But there is another feature. Suppose a teacher

is allowed to take a large number of books from a public library, display them in the school-room, and allow the scholars to rummage freely among them and select such as they like to take home to read, care having been taken by the teacher to acquaint himself with the best literature for children, and opportunities being afforded him to consult with the librarian, who, it may be, has a large knowledge of children's literature; suppose a teacher to be thus situated, to have interest enough to inform himself in regard to what are really the good books for children, and ample opportunities in the library to obtain those books and place them before the children; suppose that work of the kind mentioned begins when the children are small, and is continued for a series of years while they remain in the public schools,— can you doubt that a teacher of tact will so interest the children that a large part of their leisure time, all the time they have for reading, will be taken up in reading good books? And can you doubt, if this course is pursued long enough and faithfully enough, that the taste of the children will improve, and that you will find after a series of years that poor books are not attractive to them?

Mr. President, I should like to speak to you of the value of a library in cultivating the imagination and the moral sense, and particularly in aiding in the cause of good morals in the community where a library is established. I have no time to do this, sir, but will hint at one argument which I should like to develop. If you find that young people are loafers or idlers and are beset with the temptations which men who are idle are influenced by,— if you find boys and girls in this condition, where the lower parts of their nature are certain to come to the front, what are you to do for them? It is a cardinal principle in philanthropy that, if you would get rid of what is bad, you must substitute for it something that is interesting and good. Now supposing you create a taste for reading, you may even make a passion for reading in young people. Supposing you make it the pleasure of people as they grow up to turn when they have leisure to reading and study as a recreation. Can anybody doubt that you are giving them an immense safeguard? A philanthropist in Boston, a lady whose name you would recognize as one of those who have been very successful in doing good work in a large city, said to me, "When I find that a person whom I am trying to influence has an interest in reading, I feel a strong hope that I can do good to that person." Now, ladies and gentlemen, if your young people, as the result of a free use of books in school and in the home, can arouse in themselves a strong interest in reading, even though they read only newspapers and magazines and good stories, what a beneficent work you are doing in awakening this interest, and giving them an occupation to which they turn spontaneously instead of becoming idle and gratifying the lower appetites of human nature!

Now, Mr. President, I ought to stop, but I have just come from the beautiful library building which Mr. Larned has given you, and I saw there a window which interested me. I cannot forget that two months ago I stood on the spot at Delftshaven where John Robinson knelt and blessed the Pilgrims, and bade them God-speed as they went on board the vessel to go first to England and then to America, to found in the Old Colony of this Commonwealth their little republic and become exemplars of mankind. A few days later I stood in Leyden, in the church where John Robinson is buried, and on the outside of that church I read the inscription on the tablet which has been placed there by the American lovers and admirers of John Robinson, who is regarded as the father of Congregationalism. On a house opposite the church I saw another tablet which announced that here was the site of the house in which Robinson lived, the house in which he preached,—for he gathered his congregation about him in his dwelling-place,—and connected with which was a garden in which there were numerous little houses in which a considerable portion of his congregation lived. It was thrilling, Mr. President, to stand there amid the things which reminded one of our Pilgrim forefathers, and to think what a work John Robinson, Edward Winslow, William Bradford, and the others had done for this country and the world.

Libraries do much, sir, in an educational way to-day through pictures. We have in our own library in Worcester a magnificent collection of the largest-sized and best photographs that can be procured in Europe, illustrating the different schools of art and objects of interest throughout Europe and Asia.

You have, sir, what pictures you can afford to have, but whatever others you get,—and I assure you that they exert a great educational influence,—whatever others you get, you have the picture of John Robinson. A noble man he was. I will not speak of his love of learning, or of the University of Leyden, close by his house, of which he was a member and with whose professors he delighted so much to associate. I would rather have you think of him as the Apostle of Righteousness, as the man who was ready to sacrifice everything for what was right, and I would recall to your minds that particular feature of his righteousness which to me makes John Robinson stand out as one of the finest types of men to be found in history. He had an open mind. He was always a student, and, whenever new light came to him, he immediately, readily, willingly, heartily, gave up old views which he had found to be incorrect.

CHAIRMAN: Few who have heard of the Charles Larned Memorial and none who have passed its portals have failed to observe the prominence of the *Robinson* name, looking out from its memorial tablet and further suggested by the illuminated window over the entrance. Some years ago the Robinsons of America awoke to the fact that they had an ancestry worth looking up; and accordingly an association was organized for that purpose. The president of that association is with us to-day, having come all the way from Gloucester to recognize and honor the spirit and motive of this occasion. I take pleasure in introducing Hon. David I. Robinson, of Gloucester.

MR. ROBINSON:

Mr. Chairman,—It is with extreme pleasure that I bring to you to-day the greetings of the Robinson kinsfolk; for the erection of the Charles Larned Memorial Building is to them of more than passing interest.

This building commemorates the name of one very dear to the heart of Mr. Larned, for the one word "mother" expresses much. She was one whose long line of honorable ancestry reaches back to the Rev. John Robinson, of Pilgrim renown: she was a worthy descendant of a worthy ancestor.

My own line of genealogy I am able to trace to Abraham Robinson, who settled at Agassquam, or Annisquam, now a part of Gloucester, on Cape Ann, in 1631; but here the link is broken, and, try as we will, we cannot definitely connect with the Rev. John Robinson, although tradition is wholly on our side. We find from the Leyden records that he had a son Isaac and a son Jacob. We think, therefore, he ought to have had a son Abraham. If he did (and tradition gives it as a fact), then that son Abraham was our ancestor, and the chain is complete.

A few weeks ago the Robinson Family Genealogical and Historical Association met at the historic spot where nearly three centuries ago the flock of Rev. John Robinson sought religious freedom on our shores. Mr. Robinson, you remember, was prevented from coming with the colony or from joining it later, on account of not obtaining the consent of the English Association which controlled the enterprise. He died before this consent could be obtained, but he cheered and counseled his flock until his death, which occurred in 1625, when a life of suffering from religious persecution, but of devotion to the cause of religious freedom, was brought to a close.

On account of his strenuous life, the reverential devotion of his followers, his fatherly care over them, and his wise counsel, we are wont to think of the Rev. John Robinson as an *aged* man, who lived beyond the allotted life of threescore years and ten; yet he died at the comparatively early age of fifty years. His life was one so full of devotion to others and of self-sacrifice as not to be measured by the flight of years,—a life which the boundless ages of eternity alone can embrace.

In the rush and turmoil of the busy world of to-day there are to a greater or less degree just such characters, which stand out in bold relief,—those who, forgetful of self and living for the good of others, are the world's benefactors, heroes and heroines in the battle of life. Every such a one is making the world better by living in it.

This thought will call vividly to mind the great life which has just come to a close in your neighboring city of Worcester, or rather which is just beginning to shine in the endless ages of eternity. Senator Hoar belonged to the state, to the nation, to the world: he belonged to that class of which I speak. He lived not for himself. Wealth, honor, title, position, were nothing to him except as he could use them for the good of others. His life was a benediction; his death a sublime transition.

Monuments do not make such men great, but they serve to remind generations to come that great men have lived.

This beautiful library building which to-day the town of Oxford receives from the hand of Mr. Charles Larned is a monument—the best, the most enduring—in memory of her who was the honored daughter and seventh descendant of one of the great characters of the sixteenth and seventeenth centuries,—the Rev. John Robinson, of Leyden.

Singing.

The Old Arm-chair.

I love it! I love it! and who shall dare
To chide me for loving that old arm-chair?
I've treasured it long as a sainted prize,
I've bedewed it with tears, and embalmed it with sighs;
'Tis bound by a thousand bands to my heart;
Not a tie will break, not a link will start.
Would ye learn the spell? — A mother sat there;
And a sacred thing is that old arm-chair!

   In childhood's hour I lingered near
   The hallowed seat, with listening ear;
   And gentle words that mother would give,
   To fit me to die and teach me to live.
   She told me shame would never betide —
   With truth for my creed and God for my guide;
   She taught me to lisp my earliest prayer,
   As I knelt beside that old arm-chair.

      I sat and watched her many a day,
      When her eye grew dim, and her locks were gray;
      And I almost worshiped her when she smiled
      And turned from her Bible to bless her child.
      Years rolled on, but the last one sped —
      My idol was shattered, my earth-star fled;
      I learned how much the heart can bear,
      When I saw her die in that old arm-chair.

CHAIRMAN: This Memorial is to be transferred to the town finished and complete in all its details, therefore, no report upon the building itself is called for. It will be open for inspection at the conclusion of these exercises, and will speak for itself. A few facts, briefly stated, however, may be of interest.

The subject was first broached to the town at its annual meeting on the 2d of April, 1900,—four and a half years ago. Seven and a half sufficed for the building of Solomon's temple, but Solomon and Hiram wrought in harmony. Four and a half years! A period marked by vicissitudes "grand, gloomy, and peculiar," and by enactments wise and *otherwise*, which have passed into local history, and need not here be recounted.

The total cost to the donor of the building, with its fixed furniture, has been upwards of $27,000,— more than two and a quarter times what he first proposed to give. For the movable furniture and incidentals about $3,000—from the funds of former benefactors—has been expended, making the total cost of the building and equipments about $30,000.

The original cost of the lot was $5,500, furnished by the town and a member of the Building Committee; while the expense of grading, walks, shrubbery, etc., increased that item to nearly $6,000, thus adding to the non-taxable but large dividend-paying property of the town approximately $36,000.

It would be more in accordance with our sense of the fitness of things for Mr. Larned, in person, to present the symbols of ownership and enjoy the heart-felt applause of the beneficiaries, but his liberality is even exceeded by his modesty; and he has begged to be excused, since his forte is "Deeds rather than Words." In deference to the wishes of others, however, to which he is not indifferent, I understand he has penned a brief note, which embodies the substance of all he could say, and will be read by our now friend, Mr. Robinson, of Gloucester.

MR. ROBINSON:

OXFORD, MASS., Oct. 5, 1904.

TO THE CITIZENS OF OXFORD AND OUR WELCOME GUESTS:

Ladies and Gentlemen,— It affords me great pleasure to meet and greet you all to-day. It is an occasion for mutual congratulations. We have a common pride in this historic old town, and the memories of my early life which I passed here have prompted me to erect upon your beautiful street the Memorial Building which we dedicate to the use and benefit of all. I am glad to do this, for the character and purpose of the structure mean much to me, and I feel assured that it will be used, enjoyed, and appreciated by you and your successors for many, many years.

In tendering, through the Building Committee, the deed* of the property with the keys to the repre-

* See page 96.

71

sentatives of the town, I wish publicly to thank all who have in any way contributed to the success of the undertaking, and especially to express my high appreciation of the gratuitous services of our Building Committee, to whose untiring exertions this happy consummation is chiefly due.

Cordially yours,

CHARLES LARNED.

CHAIRMAN: "*Exegi monumentum ære perennius*," cried the enraptured Latin poet, as he contemplated his triumphs in verse,—"*I have reared a monument more lasting than brass*,"—and ages have proved it no vain boast. There are other earthly pledges of immortal honor no less sure. An *American* poet whose laurels, like those of Horace, will be green through the centuries,—James Russell Lowell,—once said on an occasion similar to the present:—

"There is no way in which a man can build so secure and lasting a monument for himself as in a public library. Upon that he may confidently allow *Resurgam* to be carved, for through his good deed he will *rise again* in the grateful remembrance and in the lifted and broadened minds and fortified characters of generation after generation. The Pyramids may forget their builders, but memorials such as this have longer memories."

And in similar strain the eloquent and lamented Henry Stedman Nourse, worthy representative of the Library Commission, thus voiced the same sentiment:—

"There is no more enduring thing, as human matters are accounted, than the free public library, and he who puts his name over its portals, either as founder or as benefactor, has built for himself a more graceful and a more enduring monument than any that his heirs can erect in any cemetery, though they pile granite skywards or with its foundations cover a rood of ground."

And so, despite all modest protests, in the far-off years when you and I shall have gone to our rest and the young life of other generations shall cluster around yon delivery desk, haply some one may ask, "Where is the resting-place of him who in the long-ago planned for us so wisely and so well, that we may at least stand in the shadow of his monument and do him honor?" And the answer shall come over seas from the silent crypt of St. Paul's, where rest the remains of its great architect, Sir Christopher Wren: *"Si monumentum quœris circumspice,"*— *"If you seek a monument, look about you,"* and the spontaneous tribute of grateful hearts shall rise like incense, and hallow all the place.

It only remains for the Building Committee to surrender its trust and responsibilities by turning over to the authorities of the town the deed of gift which, as Mr. Larned's representative, I hold in my hand, with the keys which give the people free access to the building and its treasures. Upon one of these keys is inscribed MASTER, which indicates that it will open the way to every room in the building. In it I see a type of the library itself in its sumptuously appointed home, which, rightly used, is a master-key to all the chambers of human knowledge. [Delivery of deed and keys to Lawrence F. Kilty, chairman of the Board of Selectmen.] Guard it well, and may the town be indulgent and *liberal* to this child of its old age, so making its future career of enlarged opportunity and increased usefulness tell upon the generations following,

"That our sons may be as plants grown up in their youth; that our daughters may be as corner-stones, polished after the similitude of a palace."

Mr. Kilty:

Mr. Chairman,—It gives me pleasure, in behalf of the people of Oxford, as their chosen representative on this occasion, to accept from your hand the keys to this new and valued acquisition by the town.

Oxford, rich in the munificence of her former sons and daughters, is again reminded of those who, in her earlier history, by lives and labors have contributed so much to the character and reputation which she now enjoys. This costly memorial places within easy reach of our people the key of knowledge and education. It dignifies town office, and it will be a just matter of pride to those intrusted with town affairs to see that the interests of the Free Public Library do not suffer at their hands, but rather that its usefulness is enhanced.

In behalf of the town I wish to extend thanks to the donor of the Charles Larned Memorial for one of the most beautiful free public library buildings in the Commonwealth.

74

The chairman of the Board of Selectmen in turn transferred the keys to the Trustees of the Free Public Library, represented by Orrin F. Joslin, chairman, who responded as follows: —

Mr. Chairman,—In behalf of the Trustees of Oxford Free Public Library I accept from you the keys of this building. In their acceptance we realize that we are taking upon ourselves a great responsibility, for on the public schools and public libraries depend in a large degree the developing, uplifting, and ennobling of future generations. We realize this fact, and pledge ourselves to untiring devotion to its best interests in every department of its work.

In order that this building may fulfill in the highest degree the purpose for which it has been erected, we would earnestly request the hearty cooperation of the citizens of Oxford, both old and young. Assured of this, we believe that this beautiful library building, given to the town by one deeply interested in its welfare, can be made a great power for good in this community.

CHAIRMAN: The prayer of dedication will now be offered by Rev. Charles M. Carpenter, of Oxford.

PRAYER.

Let us unite our hearts in prayer.

O Lord our God, Thou art from everlasting to everlasting. Thy days change not, Thy years are ever the same. And so we know, we are conscious, fully conscious, that Thou dost still love Thy children, and that Thou dost bestow upon the sons of men great gifts. Heaven and earth are full of them. The heavens declare Thy glory, and the earth speaks forth Thy handiwork, and yet they cannot tell us all the things Thou wouldst have us know as Thy sons and Thy daughters, created in Thine own image; and so Thou hast moved mightily upon man, and Thou hast inspired great minds to record great events, and record the noble thoughts which are born of God. And we praise Thee that generation after generation are the recipients of Thy bounty in this direction. We praise Thee, O Infinite God, that as the days come and go, ripening into centuries, the events which have gone to make up this great world's history, the events which have gone to ennoble and purify and lift up man, have been treasured by movable types and upon papers and parchments that are enduring.

And we bless Thee also that Thou didst move upon mighty men to come to this land, barren, destitute, gloomy, forbidding, and to establish here the republic that should endure as long as time endures. We praise Thee that in the hearts of these noble men there was the desire to worship the everlasting God, and to bring up generations that should honor Him forever and forever. And now we praise Thee that Thou didst send to these shores representatives of a man whose heart was full of the knowledge of the Lord, and who cried out for *more light*. May that be the petition of all descendants of him who loved his own land, but sought for his own people a larger heritage. And we pray that these generations now existing may rise, and in his memory do their best for this our beloved land. And we thank Thee for the memory of her who looked back through generations to him who loved his God and who loved his native land, and who desired for his people better things. We thank Thee for that spirit of philanthropy which she fostered in him who has so wonderfully blessed this town. We thank Thee for this donor to our Free Public Library, who has made a home for that collection which has so long been dear to this people.

We thank Thee for the hearts that inspired men and women to plant this library here in our midst. And so, Lord, we beseech Thee for Thy blessing upon all who have in any way contributed to this great event in the history of Oxford. We pray for Thy blessing upon all donors. We pray for Thy blessing upon all who have arduously toiled. We pray for Thy blessing upon the recipients of this gift. We pray for Thy blessing upon the generations yet to come and to enjoy these things. We pray for Thy benediction upon all that pertains in any way to this acquisition to our town's wealth. Hear us, we entreat Thee, and, as we dedicate this building to Thee and to Thy glory, we would dedicate it to these fathers and these mothers, these sons and these daughters; we would dedicate it to the children of generations yet unborn; we would dedicate it as a memorial forever.

And we beseech Thee to hear our petitions and

give us "more light" until the day when Thou shalt gather us all into Thy kingdom, with Jesus Christ, our Lord. Amen.

CHAIRMAN: Friends, this is, in character, a kind of "Old Home Week" gathering. Most of those who have participated are in some manner connected with Oxford, if not residents. The Orator of the Day, however, we regret to say, is a native neither of Oxford nor of Worcester County. If he were, we could not claim him, for he belongs to the nation and the age. We are, nevertheless, no less happy to welcome him here to-day, and I take great pleasure as I have the honor to introduce to you the distinguished gentleman who will deliver the dedicatory address for this occasion,

HON. CARROLL D. WRIGHT, *President of Clark College* of Worcester.

ADDRESS.

Dreams, books, are each a world ; and books, we know,
Are a substantial world, both pure and good.
Round these, with tendrils strong as flesh and blood,
Our pastime and our happiness will grow.
WORDSWORTH, *in " Personal Talk," Stanza* 3.

In books lies the soul of the whole Past Time; the articulate audible voice of the Past, when the body and material substance of it has altogether vanished like a dream.
CARLYLE, *Heroes and Hero-worship.*

The Commonwealth of Massachusetts has the proud distinction of being the only State in the world that can announce the great fact that every city and town within its borders has the right and privilege of a free public library. The importance of this proclamation is enhanced by the fact that there are 353 cities and towns in the State. One might ask why it is that this Commonwealth of ours has achieved this great work. I think we may look for an answer in the principles involved in the settlement of the Plymouth and Massachusetts Bay Colonies, notwithstanding the diversity of the characteristics of the settlers or founders of the two colonies. Those of the Plymouth Colony took on the freedom of thought of the Independents who made up the body of Pilgrims, on the one hand,— religious, broad-minded men and women as they were,— while, on the other, the men and women that made up the Massachusetts Bay Colony were Puritanical, dogmatic, narrow, proscriptive, but thoroughly imbued with the idea of the observance of a strict religious life, accompanied by the desire and the determination to secure educational privileges, the latter being evidenced by their establishment of Harvard College at an early date. There seemed to be two lines of thought in the two colonies almost antagonistic in their nature, yet running along in other directions on parallel lines. The basis of their new civilization was the church, as evidenced by the parish, the unit of municipal organization. Out of this there naturally grew the desire to establish the two fundamental elements of American civilization,— the church and, by its side, the schoolhouse. Intolerant as they were of religious free-

dom for others, fighting for the liberty of conscience,— and by that they meant the liberty of
their own conscience and not that of others,— they,
nevertheless, established those institutions and in-
sisted upon those elements of civilization which have
marked the course and the progress of this Commonwealth, and which have had an enduring influence in the establishment of American constitu-
tions. Religious to the extreme of bigotry, and
dogmatic and intolerant as they were, they were
nevertheless statesmen in a large sense, and so
ordered their lives that they have reflected on all
other political organizations in this country the firm
principles of political liberty and the loftiest ideals
of statecraft.

The leader of the Pilgrims, standing in their midst
in Holland on the 21st day of July, 1620, gave
to the world a new Magna Charta, when he said : " I
charge you if God should reveal anything to you
by any other instrument of his, be as ready to
receive it as ever you were to receive any truth
by my ministry, and I am confident that the Lord
hath more light and truth yet to break forth out
of his holy word." It was not immediately that
his disciples saw the force of this utterance. In
fact, it was not until after generations that the real
import of John Robinson's foresight was understood
by the people of the New World; but the new and
the other light came gradually, however, and the
growth of our new civilization can date its birth
from the utterances of John Robinson, whose descendant, in his generosity, and with a clear under-

standing of the necessity of intellectual growth to secure the highest ethical results, establishes this beautiful memorial as the receptacle for the public library of this ancient municipality. No other town has the satisfaction of receiving a public library erected to the memory of a lineal descendant of the Rev. John Robinson of Leyden. Your town appreciates this generosity, and more,— it appreciates the opportunity given it for perpetuating not only the memory of the one who gives it, but the lofty sentiments of the ancestor who did so much to inspire the growth of the highest qualities of mind in our Commonwealth.

You have struggled here to gain a library for the benefit of your citizens. As I read your history, I find that several attempts were made to secure a collection of books that should be of service to your citizens, and from these small beginnings you finally established a public library. But you needed a case, and Charles Larned has furnished it, and so well has he done in its furnishing that you may justly be proud of the rank you now take as the owner of one of the most beautiful library buildings in the State.

When we undertake to grasp the vast domain of knowledge, we often regret that it cannot be bequeathed as can other possessions; that the men who have spent their lives in the pursuit of some department of human knowledge or have sacrificed all comfort for the attainment of science should not be permitted to transmit their acquisitions. In our short-sightedness we feel that the world loses in some way from its sum of information when such men as Agassiz are called from their labors. This feeling of loss has taken possession of the minds of men in all the ages that have witnessed the development of the human race, and the desire to give to the world that which has been dearly won in the varied fields of learning has induced scholars to put into books the gems of their possessions.

To transmit the results of research, to record the deeds of men, to sing the praises of heroes, even to perpetuate the names of men,— these are motives which have stimulated the labor of book-writing from the days of papyrean records to present times. And yet the origin of books cannot be traced. How can it be traced when the scholastic Greek lost all tradition of the birth of his nation? And books existed long before the birth of the Greek nation. The Scriptures were written in language dead even at the time of their discovery; but the grand literature of the times of Moses and the Prophets has found in modern scholarship the most correct interpreters.

The knowledge of the past has been bequeathed to us, and we in turn shall bequeath the accumulations of all the ages to those succeeding. To bequeath the intellectual treasures of the past necessitated the institution of libraries, and so we read of the collection of books as among the earliest works of man. Even the Assyrians and Babylonians had what have been aptly designated "libraries of clay," being collections of inscribed bricks and tiles.

It is contended by some authors that the Hebrews

were the originators of libraries proper, and that the care they took for the preservation of their sacred records and the story of the actions of their ancestors furnished an example to other nations. It is recorded that Osymandyas, an Egyptian king, taking the hint from the Hebrews, established a library in his palace. He had inscribed over the door of his library, "The Storehouse of Medicine for the Mind." The Ptolemies were not only curious as to books, but preserved them in magnificence in the city of Alexandria. It was, indeed, a library that Nehemiah instituted in the temple of Jerusalem, and in which he preserved the books of the Prophets and of David, and the letters of the kings. The first public library at Athens was founded by Pisistratus. Rome had its great collections of intellectual treasures, and in ancient times every large church had its library, the first church library having been founded by Pope Nicholas at the Vatican in 1450.

The invention of the art of printing, which followed the revival of learning in the fourteenth and fifteenth centuries, of course led to a wonderful increase in the production of books, and consequently to a new era in the history of public libraries, until to-day the grandest monuments of civilization man has been able to erect are the vast libraries of the world.

So it seems that the library, almost coeval with man, certainly with the growth of acquired knowledge, has given the means for bequeathing that knowledge, and thus rendered the sacrifices of the devotees of science and of all learning the direct inheritance of all who may inquire as to the nature of their inheritance, but to none others than those who knock at the door. The history of libraries shows, of course, that ever-varying fortune which attends the history of art and of all that belongs to man's finer development, but the library has been the door which wise men have erected everywhere at which the seeker after knowledge can knock for admittance; and the only condition has been the existence of the desire to learn. How many have wanted to enter, but could find no door! How many have recognized the portal, but have failed to give the sign!

A generation before our Revolution a young man, a Boston boy, who had run away from his apprenticeship to a printer in Boston and had made his home in Philadelphia, and who had felt the great want of books, determined to institute means by which he and others like him could have the benefit of the brains of men who had recorded the results of their labor. This young man had been obliged to beg and borrow books; had pinched his stomach, that his mind might expand. The members of a little club to which he belonged contributed the few books they each owned to a common stock, and with these and a subscription of two pounds each and ten shillings a year from about fifty young men Franklin inaugurated his first important movement for the good of his fellow-men. He laid the foundation of the Public Library of Philadelphia. Franklin, in his Autobiography, in speaking of this enterprise, says: " This was the mother of all the North American subscription libraries, now so numerous. It has become a great thing itself, and continually goes on increasing. These libraries have improved the general conversation of the Americans, made the common tradesmen and farmers as intelligent as most gentlemen from other countries, and perhaps have contributed in some degree to the stand so generally made throughout the colonies in defence of their privileges."

The importance Franklin attached to this institution was great indeed, and the realization of the value of the library resulting from his own wants only influenced him still more in urging its foundation. While the creation of this subscription library at Philadelphia was, as I have said, and according to Edward Everett's testimony given at the dedication of the Boston Public Library, Franklin's first work of importance to his fellow-men, the library he established was the first of the kind of which there is any record. It was not only the mother of subscription libraries, but the parent of the distinctly American free city and town libraries which exist all over our country.

Andrew Carnegie, who has given several hundred libraries to different municipalities, has testified that he was induced to take this course through the desire in early life to have access to books, and, when a friend loaned him works from his own library, he resolved that, if he ever had the means, he would do all in his power to secure like privileges for others seeking like advantages.

This matter of bequeathing knowledge through

books and through collections of books called libraries is well illustrated by an anecdote related by Mr. Samuel S. Green, librarian of the Free Public Library of Worcester, in his address at the opening of the library building of Clark University last January. Mr. Green was undertaking to show how students seeking to add to the sum of human knowledge must, in order to prevent a waste of time and energy, first learn what is already known. Hence the need of libraries to serve as storehouses of the records of existing knowledge. He stated that the process by which civilization grows, in so far as it is advanced by the use of books, is a simple one, and that this is obvious even to the untutored savage, as is well illustrated by the remarks of Geronimo, an Indian prisoner of the United States a few years ago, who, when asked, " Do not the products of civilized life astonish you?" replied, " No, I see how they come about. A man does something, and writes a book to describe it. Another man comes along, and reads that book, and it occurs to him that he can do better the thing that has been done. He improves upon his predecessor, and writes a book to record his accomplishment. A third person improves upon the work of the second, and succeeding scholars and thinkers, adding their own achievements to those of their predecessors, in time produce the glorious results of high civilization. But," he added, " I was taken to New Orleans, and shown an establishment in which ice was made. At one end of a building I saw wood thrown into furnaces, and out of the other end came blocks of ice. Man did not do that:

only God Almighty can make ice from fire." And Mr. Green added, after relating this interesting anecdote, that, although Geronimo had not come to understand fully the power of man when he avails himself of the forces of the universe, he certainly had grasped an underlying principle in the process of civilization. The garnered treasures of past learning and the knowledge of the present are stepping stones to higher achievements and greater enlightenment. Standing on the shoulders of earlier scholars, we gain a wider outlook and broader views.

So we need have no fear of losing the results of the work accomplished by the human intellect. The man who accomplishes results is mortal, and dies, but his work survives him, and the library is the storehouse that perpetuates all that is worth remembering and what the student needs to enable him to go forward in his researches, while it furnishes the opportunity to man to gain a broader culture in life, even if he does not secure the fundamental facts of knowledge. Literature, art, everything that helps to adorn the human character, can be gained by reading, — by the study of what is and of what has been.

So the library is what Carlyle called it. He said, " The true university of these days is a collection of books." That author, given to epigrammatic sayings, never recorded a wiser one. The library is the university of the town, and every town in our honored Commonwealth has this university. It is the source to which all citizens can freely go whenever taste, inclination, or the desire for knowledge, inspires them. And in the light of this grand influence we may overlook the criticisms that are often made upon the character of the collection. This world is not made up entirely of wheat. In the divine plan there is chaff. The thistles will grow up and help smother the pure grain, but the pure grain is there, and the care exercised by the managers of our public libraries is evidence that the tares are kept to the minimum.

The influence of the library as the university of the town is felt to a large degree in the new processes or new methods, rather, of instruction. Many of us remember that the teacher's task as a teacher was finished when she had asked the questions at the bottom of the page of the text-book; that there was no indication or suggestion of what the student better read in a collateral way in order to interest him and to enable him to gain other information than that given in the text-book, or to broaden his mind by understanding the views of other authors than those given him to study. In fact, there would have been little use fifty years ago of the teacher's suggesting to the student a course of collateral reading, for the source of such reading was not at hand, except in a very few private libraries, and then only to a limited degree. Now the teacher knows well that putting the questions which the text-book contains is the smallest or slightest part of her work. She must illuminate the whole subject; she must stimulate the young mind in its plastic stage; she must throw around her work the elements that will induce the boy or girl to seek further light and to secure greater enjoyment in the acquisition of knowledge. If it be a class in history, she can easily say to its members, "You will find in such and such works an elaboration of this principle or the facts given more *in extenso*," and the pupil has recourse to the public library, where he can supplement the somewhat rigid work of the curriculum by interesting collateral reading and gain a new insight into the dryness of the text-book.

This course leads the young mind to comprehend the real power of knowing well what is taught in a preliminary way only in the public schools. The pupil learns the power which he gains by a fuller knowledge, and, if he be industrious and his selections are wise, he can lead his class, and be an influence in his school and in his community. While this is peculiarly true of history, it is also true that other branches afford the same opportunity—in different degrees, perhaps—of acquiring that collateral knowledge which is so necessary in the study of any branch of learning.

Truly, the public library is the university of the town, but it goes beyond this. The use of the books of a public library by the pupils in the schools carries its influence to the father and the mother and the older members of the family, and a taste for reading is acquired. Those of us who are passing down the closing years of our lives know well that the man who has a taste for reading, who never allows an hour to pass in idleness when he can occupy himself with a good book, has a hold that no other man has. He is not only entertaining himself, but he may entertain others; and he is a safer man, a better citizen, a truer patriot, than the man who has never had the good fortune to acquire the taste for reading. The library helps him in his declining years to make himself an agreeable companion and a real helper in the progress of the studies of the youth of his community.

We often hear some condemnation of the public library. You will recall that the distinguished playwright, Richard Brinsley Sheridan, in "The Rivals," puts it in the mouth of one of his characters to say that "a circulating library in a town is as an evergreen tree of diabolical knowledge." This sentiment was uttered 130 years ago, but we still hear it. We are still told that the public library feeds the ambition of the young, causes degeneration of the mind, and pollutes morals; and here and there we hear of a youth who has been led into criminal courses by reading trashy novels and adventures. We hear that much reading creates discontent among the people, who, it is assumed, ought to confine their lives in the narrow limits of a workaday existence; that through this discontent they are constantly grasping for things not within their reach, and that by such grasping they fail to perform the duties belonging to an industrious life.

All these things may be true, but I assure you they are true only in a very limited degree; and the extent to which they are true is offset by a higher element which comes into the lives of those who have free access to books. Every day I meet men of the strongest mental capacity, men hard at work in their particular walk in life—students of science, writers, men whose labors cannot be limited to an eight or a ten hour day,—the products of whose minds are giving to the world some of the best thought and the best results that can be secured, but who seek recreation, relaxation,—rest, in fact,— by reading romance. We may say this is perfectly safe for a mature mind, but unsafe for the young. I believe too much novel-reading by the young is pernicious to some degree, but chiefly because it may vitiate a taste for reading of a higher order. The good, clean, and wholesome novel only stimulates mental activity: it does not dull it; but, carried too far, the better works are laid aside or neglected, just as too much magazine reading after a while vitiates the taste or dulls the desire to read more sustained works. A man who reads magazines constantly, shrinks from taking up a work of four or five hundred pages on some subject which would be of advantage to him. And yet the magazine is the chief source to which many in their busy lives can turn for the gratification of the desire to read at all. The skimming of newspapers—a necessity in our day—takes the edge off the desire to read books. But, when we study the statistics of libraries and see the character of the works that circulate in any community, especially in New England, I think one is fully satisfied that there are no works of substantial merit in a public library that do not receive gratifying attention.

We are living in the day when competition is mind with mind. Life is exacting. The necessity to earn one's living and to support one's family leads to the desire for recreation, and this modern condition superinduces the desire for general reading. The activity of the mind must be fed, and the degree in which the feeding process goes on depends upon the facility of securing the food.

I believe that the reading by any man or boy or girl of even what we may call trashy novels is better for him or her than the idling away of his or her life on the street or in questionable places, though by such reading we may occasionally witness a wreck. In every work there will be found something good, and, if a book takes a boy off the street and from vicious companions, so much good has been accomplished. The influence may not be immediate, but it is there. It is always in every book, as in every play, however low down it may be, that virtue is lauded, and when virtue triumphs, even in the old Bowery Theatre in New York, the applause which comes from the galleries is stronger than that from any other part of the house; and no author of a cheap novel would allow his created villain to secure permanent success. Many a child reading light and even frivolous works has often had his taste for reading stimulated to the selection of better books, and this process may secure to him that general taste for reading which enables one to obtain higher positions in life than would otherwise have been possible. There is no one so poor as the man who does not read.

We must not condemn utterly all reading simply because some is of such a character as to exert a bad influence. This is just as true of life as it is of books. We must not condemn all men because some are vicious. The better way to overcome the influences which come from strong drink is by some healthful substitute. It may not be a radical substitute, but whatever it is that prevents the presence in the saloon or the idling away of hours in the streets in dissolute companionship is certainly to be commended, in so far as it accomplishes this result.

But there is one grand satisfaction in considering this side of the public library, and that is that in the sterling virtues of our people, as exercised through the town meeting, the purest type of democracy that has ever existed, there is a careful scrutiny in the selection of books for the shelves. This must be kept up. There must be a judicious censorship in the management of every public library, and with this censorship we need have no very alarming fears of the result.

I think it is safe to say that the public library now completes the trinity of public influences in shaping thought. Our forefathers established the church and the school-house. We have added to these the public library, and now these three great institutions are with us, and aim for the very best civilization. How can it be otherwise? What has been the great influence that keeps this country true to the principles established by the settlers? We are not a warlike people. We believe in education, and are willing to take the results. France, with its brilliant history, with all its science and its literature, now spends $4 per capita for military purposes per annum, and only 70 cents per capita for general public educational work; and England, our mother, spends $3.72 per annum for military purposes, and only 62 cents per capita for the education of her people. Prussia spends $2.04 for her military establishment per capita, and only 50 cents for her public schools. The United States expends 75 cents per capita per annum for military equipment, and $3 per capita for her public education, while we in Massachusetts spend $4.96 for every man, woman, and child within the State's borders for public schools.

These facts testify to the influences which have worked with us. They show that we care more for the qualities of the mind than for any other, and that we are following the great exhortation of John Robinson to receive light whenever it is revealed to us; and this library, citizens of Oxford, this generous memorial, is an evidence that in your triple position of Pilgrim and Puritan and Huguenot you have not lost sight of those great principles which mean religious and political liberty and intellectual freedom.

CHAIRMAN: Permit me to repeat the notice already given, that the Charles Larned Memorial will be open for inspection at the close of these exercises.

You are now requested to rise and join in the singing of " America, " and remain standing until the benediction is pronounced by Rev. Albert Tyler, of Oxford.

America.

BENEDICTION.

And now may the Father's everlasting blessing rest upon this edifice which we have upon this occasion dedicated. May the Father's kindly hand rest in blessing upon the head and heart of him who was inspired to build it. May the memories of this glorious occasion be with us in days to come, inspiring us to work for humanity and for the glory of God. Amen.

DEED.

Know all men by these presents,

That I, **CHARLES LARNED**, *of Boston, in the County of Suffolk and Commonwealth of Massachusetts, in consideration of one dollar and other valuable considerations paid by the* **TOWN OF OXFORD**, *in the County of Worcester and Commonwealth of Massachusetts, the receipt whereof is hereby acknowledged, do hereby remise, release, and forever* quitclaim *unto the said* **TOWN OF OXFORD** *a building constructed of Kittanning gray brick with Milford pink granite foundation and trimmings, designated on a granite slab at the front of the balcony over the main entrance and known as the* **CHARLES LARNED MEMORIAL**, *for the purpose set forth on a metal tablet set into the front wall in a niche north of said main entrance, bearing the following legend:*

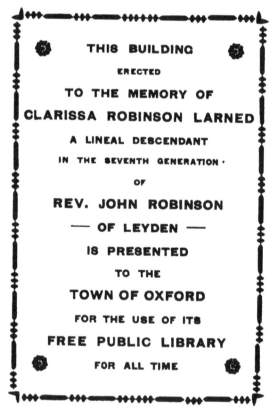

THIS BUILDING

ERECTED

TO THE MEMORY OF

CLARISSA ROBINSON LARNED

A LINEAL DESCENDANT

IN THE SEVENTH GENERATION ·

OF

REV. JOHN ROBINSON

— OF LEYDEN —

IS PRESENTED

TO THE

TOWN OF OXFORD

FOR THE USE OF ITS

FREE PUBLIC LIBRARY

FOR ALL TIME

Said building being located on what was formerly known as the " Captain De Witt lot" and later as the " Hyde lot," on the west side of Main Street, at the corner of Sigourney Street, in said

Oxford, bounded and described as follows: on the east by Main Street about one hundred seventy-five feet; on the north by land of Orrin F. Joslin about two hundred feet; on the west by land of Herman H. Sigourney about one hundred seventy-five feet; on the south by Sigourney Street about two hundred feet; being the same premises conveyed to Orrin F. Joslin by Mary D. Hyde by deed dated the twenty-third day of July in the year one thousand nine hundred one (23 July, 1901) and recorded in Worcester District Registry Book 1690, page 444, corrected by a quitclaim deed from said Hyde to said Joslin, dated 20 May, 1902, and filed for record in Worcester District Registry.

To have and to hold the granted premises, with all the privileges and appurtenances thereto belonging, to the said Town of Oxford and its heirs and assigns, to their own use and behoof forever.

And I do hereby, for myself and my heirs, executors, and administrators, covenant with the said grantee and its heirs and assigns that the granted premises are free from all incumbrances made or suffered by me, and that I will and my heirs, executors, and administrators shall warrant and defend the same to the said grantee and its heirs and assigns forever against the lawful claims and demands of all persons claiming by, through, or under me, but against none other.

In witness whereof, I, the said **CHARLES LARNED**, being unmarried, hereunto set my hand and seal this twenty-ninth day of September in the year one thousand nine hundred and four.

Signed, sealed, and delivered }
    in presence of   }   **CHARLES LARNED.** [SEAL]
JOHN E. KIMBALL.   }

Commonwealth of Massachusetts

Suffolk ss., 29 September, 1904. Then personally appeared the above-named **CHARLES LARNED,** and acknowledged the foregoing instrument to be his free act and deed, before me,

JOHN E. KIMBALL,

Worcester, ss.   Justice of the Peace.

November 15, 1904, at 3 hours, 16 minutes, p.m. Received and entered with Worcester District Deeds, Book 1794, page 487.

Attest:

DANIEL KENT,

Register.

97

THE BUILDING.

The plot upon which the Charles Larned Memorial stands is the most eligible, for library purposes,
within the limits of the town. Sufficiently removed
from the noisy activities of village life, it is yet
hard-by the business and residential centre and
within easy reach of post-office, stores, schools, and
churches.

"Oxford Plain," so called, is noted for the beauty
of its Main Street. Seven rods in width, this well-
shaded thoroughfare extends north and south for
nearly a mile on a level.

Upon its west side with a frontage of about
180 feet and a depth westward of 200 feet on
Sigourney Street,— its southern boundary,— bordered on the north and west by private estates, these
amply shaded and spacious grounds, retired, yet easy
of access, offer an ideal location for an institution
upon which more than upon any other is focussed
the interest of the whole community.

The building, in the form of a Roman cross and
Renaissance in style of architecture, is placed in the
centre of the lot, facing eastward, the extreme
width from north to south being about 70 feet, and
its length, east and west from entrance steps to rear
of stack-room, upwards of 82 feet.

CHARLES WEST COPE, R.A.

BORN

1811, in Leeds, England

DIED

August, 1890, at Bournemouth, England

"The Departure of the Pilgrims from Holland in 1620"

Painted in 1856

THIS TABLET
ERECTED
TO THE MEMORY OF
CLARISSA ROBINSON LARNED
A LINEAL DESCENDANT
EIGHTH GENERATION
FROM
REV. JOHN ROBINSON
—— OF LEYDEN ——
IS PRESENTED
TO THE
TOWN OF OXFORD
FOR THE USE OF ITS
FREE PUBLIC LIBRARY
FOR ALL TIME.

The central portion is two stories in height, affording a spacious room on the second floor for the display of art and antiquities, small gatherings for conference, a trustees' room, attic storage rooms, etc.

A broad granolithic walk leads from Main Street to the front entrance,— the head of the cross,—and, ascending a flight of eight granite steps flanked by heavy buttresses, we stand in the entrance porch between polished granite columns and pilasters. Over our heads, in heavy block letters cut from the solid stone, stands out

FREE PUBLIC LIBRARY,

and surmounting this, in front of the balcony above,

CHARLES LARNED
MEMORIAL,

while just to the right of the porch, in a niche corresponding to the window on the left, is placed a massive bronze tablet, bearing the legend reproduced on page 96.

Entering the vestibule, a flight of stairs on the right leads to the basement. Passing through the door in front, we are in the Delivery Hall. On the right, stairs lead to the floor above. On the left is a small room furnished with cases, table, and chairs for special study or conversation. Directly in front is the Delivery Counter and Cataloguing Room, immediately in the rear of which is the Stack Room. On the right or north of the delivery counter is the Librarian's Room, with Toilet Room adjoining. Corresponding to the librarian's room on the left or south of the delivery counter is the Reference Room. South of the delivery hall and reference room and extending from front to rear of the main building is the General Reading Room, lighted by windows on three sides. In the corresponding wing on the north side is the Juvenile Room, somewhat smaller. Each of the two latter being furnished with a spacious fireplace, bordered by enamelled tile-work and a rich mantel.

The stack-room, including the basement, is designed for three tiers of stacks, with a total capacity for 40,000 volumes, and is practically fireproof, being separated from the main building by fireproof walls and doors. Between the stack-room and main structure there are outside stairways leading up to the cataloguing room — being the rear entrance connected with Sigourney Street by a granolithic walk — and down to the basement, which with its whitened walls and cement flooring is spacious and well lighted, affording accommodation for the steam-heating apparatus, coal bunkers, toilet and storage rooms, and any additional equipment which may be required in the future. The building is heated by steam and is piped for gas, though lighted throughout by electricity, and supplied with running water from a neighboring hill.

The building material is Milford pink granite and a light gray brick. The ashlar basement, including water-table, steps, and entrance porch entire, door and window sills and caps, chimney caps and coping, are of selected granite, while the brick of which the walls are constructed is from Kittanning, Armstrong County, Pa., and so thoroughly vitrified in the process of manufacture as to be impervious to moisture.

The roof of the main structure is covered with Monson black slate, trimmed with copper hip, ridge crestings, and finials, and that of the stack-room with rolled copper. The floors of the first and second story are of kiln-dried quartered oak, the general reading, reference, and juvenile rooms having inlaid patterns, except those of the delivery hall and vestibule, which are Italian marble mosaic, flecked with the French fleur-de-lis, with ornamental border of classic design, the base-boards, plinths, and thresholds being of the same rich material, while in the centre of the space a graceful wreath incloses the monogram of Mrs. Larned, for whom the building stands as a memorial.

The stack-room is exceptionally well lighted and well ventilated, with ample windows upon three sides, and furnished with Library Bureau clutch double steel stack, glass floor, hand lift, and iron stairway.

The walls and ceilings are tastefully tinted and decorated, while the interior finish, with all furniture, fixed and movable, designed and made to order, is of choice quartered oak, finished in natural tints.

One of the most artistic features of the structure is the stained glass work of Redding, Baird & Co., Boston. While plain, polished plate glass, from considerations of utility, was adopted for windows, doors, and sometimes partitions, the leaded glass bordering the main doorway, transoms, and especially the large arched window over the porch appeal strongly to the æsthetic sense, and are notable for their appropriateness and artistic merit. The latter commemorates "The Departure of the Pilgrims from Holland in 1620," and represents a group from the famous painting of Charles West Cope, R.A., one of a series decorating the British House of Parliament.

This superb creation, about eight by ten feet in size, consists of a large central panel surrounded by border panels at the top and sides, with emblematic medallions representing "The Mayflower," "The Open Bible," and "A Burning Lamp," which serve as foils to the main group.

The central figure of the devout circle kneeling at the water's edge is that of the revered Robinson, with outstretched arms and eyes turned heavenward as he commits his charge to Him who rules the winds and waves. The accessories are in the highest degree suggestive, especially the local coloring, as seen in the Dutch dwellings of gray stone with heavy gables and tiled roofs, the old windmill, the waiting boat ready to convey its precious freight to the "Mayflower" in the offing, and even the pastor's passionate soul-cry for "More Light" flashing forth in ruby and gold from the clear skies overhead.

The transoms on the main floor, including the stairway, each of which is a work of art, are no less noticeable for their suggestive beauty. In the centre of each is a twelve-inch circular medallion,

THE DEPARTURE OF THE PILGRIMS FROM HOLLAND IN 1620.
CHARLES WEST COPE, R.A.

twelve being reproductions of old book-marks used by printers and publishers, mostly in the sixteenth century, while the remaining four in the juvenile room consist of flowers and figures selected from "Flora's Feast" by Walter Crane.

They may be briefly described as follows: —

SPECIAL STUDY ROOM.

Arion with violin and bow, standing upon the dolphin.
Johann Oporin, *Basle.*
About 1510–1570.

An anchor held by two hands and bearing the Greek letters Alpha and Omega, also Chi Rho, the initial letters of the name of "The Anointed."
Motto: " CONCORDIA."
Gerardus Wolfschatius, *Antwerp.*
About 1601–1625.

GENERAL READING ROOM.

A crab below, a butterfly above.
Motto: " MATURA."
Jehan Trellon, *Lyons,* and other Lyons printers.
About 1540–1550.

An anchor held by a hand reaching from the clouds.
Motto: " ANCHORA SPEI."
Thomas Vautrollier, *London and Edinburgh.*
About 1565–1605.
Also
John Norton, *London.*
1601–

A primitive hand-press and an open book, surrounded by a ring of serpents.   Invented 1428, 1440.

Copied from a silver medal struck in Haarlem by Laurens Koster.

A pair of compasses directed by a hand.
Motto: " LABORE ET CONSTANTIA."

The best known of several devices used by the famous Plantins of Antwerp, printers and publishers.   Introduced by Christopher Plantin about 1550.

Pegasus.
Motto: " AD ASTRA VOLANDUM."
Jeremiah Duemlerus, *Nuremberg.*
About 1601–1650.

The winged bust of a woman with three heads,—a woman, an old man, a young man.   A laurel wreath above, a star in the woman's forehead, an open book below.
Motto: " USUS ME GENUIT."
Melchior and Gaspard Trechsel, *Lyons.*
About 1526–1550.

REFERENCE ROOM.

A Bible richly bound, in a circle of light.
Motto: " VETAT MORI."
David Martini, *Antwerp.*
About 1601.

LIBRARIAN'S ROOM.

An open book displayed on the breast of Phœnix, bearing the Greek letters Alpha and Omega.
Motto: " RENOVABITUR."
Johannes Columbius, *Deventer.*
About 1650.

STAIRWAY.

A boy piping beneath a tree beside a stream on which he has just launched a tiny boat bearing a burning lamp.

Motto: " TOUT BIEN OU RIEN."

Elihu Vedder's design for the Riverside Press, Cambridge, first made to accompany his illustrations to " Rubáiyat " of Omar Khayyám.

Two hands holding upright a caduceus, on which is perched a bird. The two serpents are crowned.

Motto: " FROBEN."

The device of John Froben, *Basle.*

About 1490–1525.

JUVENILE ROOM.

The Tulips lift their banners red,
Or fill their cups with fire instead.

The little Crocus reaches up
To catch a sunbeam in his cup.

The evening Primrose lights her lamp,
A beacon to the garden camp.

The Lilies of the day are done,
And sunk the golden westering Sun.

Those who have been instrumental in realizing an expression of the sentiment and purpose which here find embodiment are : —

Cutting, Carleton & Cutting,
  Worcester . . . . ARCHITECTS.
Rankin & Woodside, *Worcester* . . . GENERAL CONTRACTORS.

O. Berggren, *Oxford* . . . . MILFORD PINK GRANITE.

Boston Fire Brick Co., *Boston* . . . . KITTANNING (PA.) GRAY BRICK.

George A. Barnard & Sons, *Worcester* . ROOFING.

Willis C. Beveridge, *Oxford* . . . . PLASTERING.

New England Marble and Mosaic Co-operative Co., *Boston* . . . . . MOSAIC WORK.

O. S. Kendall & Son, *Worcester* . . . HEATING AND TILE WORK.

Redding, Baird & Co., *Boston* . . . STAINED GLASS.

Stenberg & Co., *Worcester* . . . . . . MURAL DECORATION.

Plummer, Ham & Richardson, *Worcester* . . . . ELECTRIC WORK.

T. F. McGann & Sons Co., *Boston* . . BRONZE TABLET.

Library Bureau, *Boston* . . . . . . FURNITURE AND FITTINGS.

Heywood Bros. & Wakefield Co., *Boston* . . . . FURNITURE.

Henry M. Pratt, *Boston* . . . . . . GRADING AND SHRUBBERY.

The Receipts and Disbursements whereby this was accomplished are best set forth in the Report of the Building Committee submitted to the town at its annual meeting, 3 April, 1905, which is hereto appended.

REPORT

OF THE

BUILDING COMMITTEE

OF THE

CHARLES LARNED MEMORIAL.

The Building Committee of the Charles Larned Memorial was appointed when the terms of the gift required that one-third of the expense should be borne by the town. Subsequently, Mr. Larned proposed to assume the entire expense of the building, and in view of this change no report to the town, save as regards the Wallace Fund and the $500 appropriation by the town, would seem to be called for, but, as the citizens are deeply interested in all details connected with our Free Public Library, the financial report of the Charles Larned Memorial, in so far as it has been determined by the Committee, is respectfully submitted.

CONTRIBUTIONS AND APPROPRIATIONS.

O. F. Joslin	$1,000.00
Town appropriation	500.00
Wallace Fund	2,783.84
Town appropriation for lot	4,500.00
Charles Larned	25,083.47
Credit allowed by town on insurance for three years,	116.65
	$33,983.96
Town appropriation of $500 overdrawn	13.83
	$33,997.79

DISBURSEMENTS.

	Lot.	Movable Furniture.	Building and Fixed Furniture.	Total Cost.
Library site	$5,500.00	—	—	$5,500.00
Telegram Newspaper Co.	13.80	—	—	13.80
George E. Chaffee, printing	4.75	—	—	4.75
J. E. Kimball, labor of teams	26.39	—	—	26.39
Vinton Bros , teams	255.58	—	—	255.58
Chaffee Bros. Co., pipes, etc.	18.10	—	—	18.10
John H. McWhorter, labor . . .	—	—	54.35	54.35
H. M. Pratt, grading and shrubs . . .	678.58	—	—	678.58
C. S. Bacon, insurance	—	—	140.00	140.00
Visiting libraries for plans	—	—	16.46	16.46
Postage, car-fare, filling post holes . . .	3.52	—	—	3.52
Stationery and telephone	—	—	.45	.45
Expense to Boston for plans	—	—	5.44	5.44
W. H. Haven, piping	—	—	28.48	28.48
William I. Thompson, engineer . . .	—	—	8.95	8.95
N. S. Pike, cleaning well	10 00	—	—	10.00
Boardman Bros., copper box	—	—	2.55	2.55
Vinton Bros., trucking	—	—	2.00	2.00
Express on tablets	—	—	3.30	3.30
Duncan & Goodell, hardware	—	—	175.00	175.00
H. O Lamson, lighting	—	—	453.00	453.00
Chaffee Bros. Co., chairs	—	$212.65	—	212.65
C F. Daniels, labor	.68	—	—	.68
The Clark-Sawyer Co , tools	—	9.06	—	9.06
Duncan & Goodell, tools	—	10.00	—	10.00
John H. McWhorter, labor	14.75	—	—	14.75
William Miller & Son. labor	26.03	—	—	26.03
Doll & Richards, framing plan	—	18.50	—	18.50
H. M. Pratt, plan	—	15.00	—	15.00
Law & Hawxhurst, gas and electric fixtures	—	—	184.00	184.00
Dedication expense, printing, etc. . . .	—	—	40.32	40.32
Expense, telephone, freight	—	.50	2.57	3.07
Freight on gas machine	—	—	6.71	6.71
Plummer, Ham & Richardson, elec. w'k .	—	—	41.40	41.40
C. G. Farnsworth, putting on door spring,	—	—	1.55	1.55
Barnard, Sumner & Putnam, curtains .	—	37.80	—	37.80
E. A. Wheelock, door spring . . .	—	—	1.80	1.80
Rankin & Woodside, contract	—	—	20,083.30	20,083.30
Rankin & Woodside, coal	—	—	13.50	13.50
O. Berggren, extra on stone work . .	—	—	453.30	453.30
Cutting, Carleton & Cutting, architects .	—	—	1,029.34	1,029.34
O. S. Kendall, heating	—	—	800.00	800.00
Library Bureau, furniture and stack-room	—	623.25	3,630.25	4,253.50
Chaffee Bros. Co , lumber, pipe, etc .	.40	6.00	7.70	14.10
Postage	—	—	8.23	8.23
	$6,552.58	$932 76	$27,193 95	$34,679.29
Lot reduced by sale of buildings	681.50	—	—	681.50
	$5,871.08			$33,997.79

The above does not include the cost of copper roof over stack-room, mosaic floor in de-livery-room, ornamental glass windows and bronze tablet, approximating $2,500, which items were paid by Mr. Larned, and of whose cost the committee has no knowledge.

JOHN E. KIMBALL,
ORRIN F. JOSLIN, } Building
ALFRED M. CHAFFEE, } Committee.

OXFORD, Mass., 3 April, 1905.

108

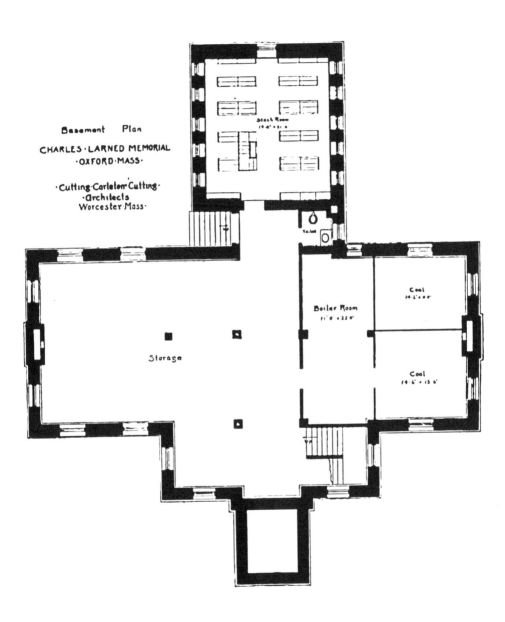

Basement   Plan

CHARLES · LARNED MEMORIAL
·OXFORD·MASS·

·Cutting·Carleton·Cutting·
·architects
Worcester Mass·

Stack Room

Toilet

Coal

Boiler Room

Coal

Storage

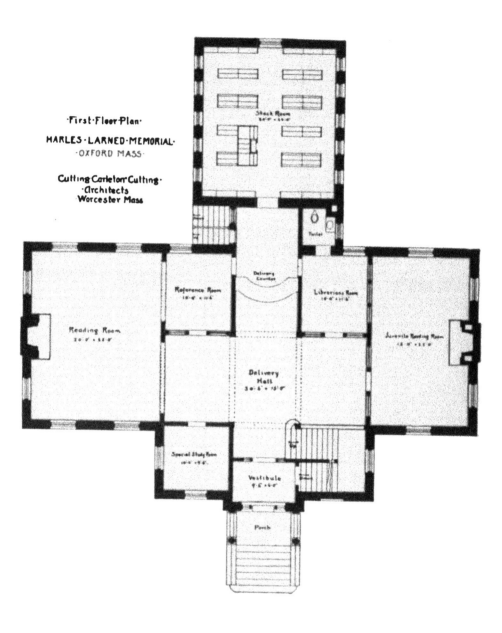

·First·Floor·Plan·

HARLES·LARNED·MEMORIAL·
·OXFORD MASS·

Cutting·Carleton·Cutting·
·Architects·
·Worcester Mass·

Stack Room

Reference Room

Delivery Counter

Librarians Room

Reading Room

Juvenile Reading Room

Delivery Hall

Toilet

Special Study Room

Vestibule

Porch

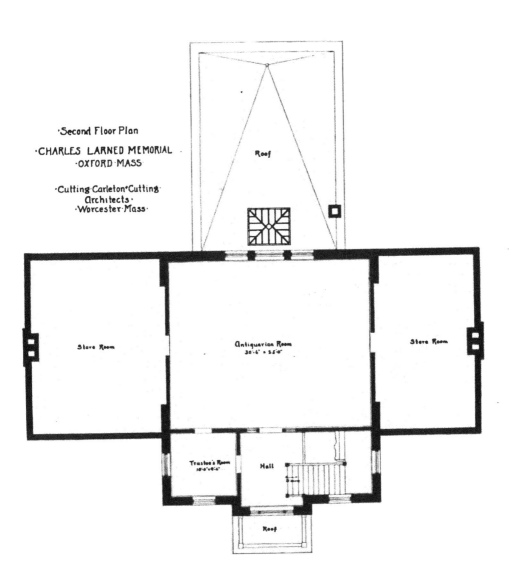

·Second Floor Plan·

·CHARLES LARNED MEMORIAL·
·OXFORD·MASS·

·Cutting·Carleton·Cutting·
·Architects·
·Worcester·Mass·

Roof

Store Room

Antiquarian Room
30'-4" × 35'-0"

Store Room

Trustee's Room
16'-0"×9'-6"

Hall

Roof

STAIRWAY LEADING TO SECOND FLOOR.

DELIVERY COUNTER AND CATALOGUING ROOM.
STACK ROOM IN REAR.
DOOR OF LIBRARIAN'S ROOM ON THE RIGHT.

LOOKING FROM JUVENILE ROOM TO GENERAL READING ROOM
ACROSS DELIVERY HALL.

LOOKING FROM GENERAL READING ROOM TO JUVENILE ROOM
ACROSS DELIVERY HALL.

A CORNER IN THE JUVENILE ROOM, LOOKING WEST.

GENERAL READING ROOM, LOOKING SOUTH.

CPSIA information can be obtained
at www.ICGtesting.com
Printed in the USA
BVHW071345231118
533754BV00029B/2734/P